IMMIGRANT EXPERIENCES

IMMIGRANT EXPERIENCES

Expanding the School-Home-Community Dialogue

Edited by Ruth McKoy Lowery, Mary Ellen Oslick, and Rose M. Pringle

ROWMAN & LITTLEFIELD
Lanham • Boulder • New York • London

Published by Rowman & Littlefield
An imprint of The Rowman & Littlefield Publishing Group, Inc.
4501 Forbes Boulevard, Suite 200, Lanham, Maryland 20706
www.rowman.com

6 Tinworth Street, London SE11 5AL

British Library Cataloguing in Publication Information Available

Library of Congress Cataloging-in-Publication Data Available

ISBN: 978-1-4758-4758-1 (cloth : alk. paper)
ISBN: 978-1-4758-4759-8 (pbk. : alk. paper)
ISBN: 978-1-4758-4760-4 (electronic)

Dedication

Ruth: For immigrant families everywhere. I salute your courage to dream of a better world!

Mary Ellen: For my children—may this dialogue strengthen the future of our nation.

Rose: For my mother, brother, and sisters, and their families, and for my husband and children—all immigrants.

CONTENTS

ACKNOWLEDGMENTS

This timely and important professional contribution would not have been possible without the support from our families, friends, and colleagues. A special thank you to Tom Koerner, whose faith in the project and encouragement kept us focused; and to the Rowman & Littlefield editorial and production teams, especially Carlie Wall and Hannah Fisher for their guidance throughout the project.

We thank the reviewers whose constructive feedback helped to make this project a reality. A very special thank you to Dr. Barbara Lehman for writing the foreword, and to Christina Levy for her original poem, "Silenced by Language." Thanks to Dr. Hasan Aydin, Dr. Jeanne G. Fain, and Dr. Deb L. Marciano for agreeing to review the manuscript and write endorsements for this book at short notice. Your faith in this project and work with diverse student populations strengthen the conversations on meeting the needs of all students.

The idea for this book was birthed after conversations with parents, scholars, and community leaders. We are excited to share the work we do as a collective, noting the timeliness of issues and discussions centering immigration on a global scale. We thank all the contributors who worked diligently on their chapters and responded in a timely manner to editorial reminders to bring this project to fruition. We are grateful for the participation of family, school, and community members who have contributed to make this project successful. We are all better for the communication and positive connections we share in working with diverse immigrant families.

LIST OF FIGURES

FOREWORD

Barbara A. Lehman

"No matter where you are from, we're glad you're our neighbor."

Probably you've seen the green, blue, and orange-gold yard sign written in three languages: English and two others, depending upon the locale. Perhaps you even have one gracing your front yard, demonstrating your acceptance of diversity and embracing newcomers to your neighborhood. Since all Americans (except for the original inhabitants of North America) are immigrants, those of us whose ancestors arrived over the last 500 or so years owe it to our own heritage to provide a hospitable land for recent arrivals. Yet, the United States—a nation of immigrants—has struggled and continues to waver between welcoming and rejecting new arrivals, often depending upon those outsiders' origins (contradicting the yard sign message) and how we perceive them.

But, in fact, here they are in significantly large numbers: legal, undocumented, and/or seeking refuge from terrors or disasters in their homelands. According to United States Census Population Survey data (2016), 13.4 percent of American residents are foreign born—a 5.5 million (or 8.7 percent) increase from 2010 to 2016 (Current Population Survey 2010, 2016)—and a reality that many, if not most, American teachers see reflected in their classrooms today. All newcomers face adjustment issues and sometimes hardships (including lack of acceptance from the native born or inadequate resources) when they arrive in a new place. No work of fiction captures better the sense of strangeness and displacement that new immigrants may feel than *The Arrival* (2006), Australian Shaun

Tan's surreal wordless narrative. Furthermore, as many as 11 to 12 million immigrants are undocumented (Estimates 2018), and their challenges can be even more daunting.

Recent policy changes of the United States government present new and shifting contexts for educators who work with immigrant students. For example, refugee quotas have been lowered to 30,000 per year starting in 2019, reduced sharply from the 85,000 accepted in 2016 (Krogstad and Radford 2017) and a tiny fraction of the 65.6 million ("On World Refugee Day" 2017) displaced persons worldwide. Or, changes in green card rules may make it harder for immigrants to obtain the services they need and to which they are entitled. Even undocumented workers contribute billions—more than $11 billion in 2016 according to Chen (2016)—in state, local, income, property, and consumer taxes and pay into Social Security. According to Vargas (2012), "immigration has become a third-rail issue in Washington, DC, because it deals with issues of race and class, of entitlement and privilege" (44). No wonder the educator's role is so complex and must necessarily involve students' homes, schools, and communities. No wonder that it is so critical for all three entities to communicate and coordinate with each other.

Journalist Warren St. John vividly chronicles a paradigm for this kind of total involvement in the lives of immigrant students, especially the refugees portrayed in *Outcasts United* (2009), a national bestseller. As literary nonfiction, it portrays a young Jordanian immigrant woman's dedication to organizing a soccer program for diverse teenage refugees in Clarkston, Georgia, a traditional Southern town in the United States. As Coach Luma Mufleh became involved in their lives, her initial focus on soccer evolved into a cause for changing their entire environment.

Clarkston is a small town in the suburbs of Atlanta that was first settled after the Civil War and remained mostly white until the 1980s when middle-class whites departed for newer suburbs farther from downtown Atlanta. They were replaced first by African American renters in Clarkston's apartment complexes and, by the end of the decade, refugees who were resettled in the United States through nonprofit agency programs. The first refugees came from Southeast Asia, then Bosnia, Kosovo, and the former Soviet Union, eventually African countries beset by war—Somalia, Sudan, Congo, Liberia, Burundi, Ethiopia, Eritrea—and recently, Afghanistan and Iraq. By the 2000 census, Clarkston's population was at least one-third foreign born, a fact that utterly changed the town (St. John 2009). This sudden diversity came at a cost, with growing resentment from old-time residents about what they regarded as the constant problems posed by the new arrivals: lack of English-language proficiency, poverty, cultural differences in mores and practices, even poor driving skills. The town government was ill-equipped to deal with these issues, and the refugee resettlement agencies were too overwhelmed and underfunded to meet the challenges.

In turn, the townspeople understood little about where these new immigrants originated or what traumatic conditions had forced them to flee their homelands, such as ethnic cleansing, civil war, famine, or brutal oppression from authorities. Many refugees deeply distrusted anyone in uniform or the government. Both sides withdrew to their own "tribes," and attitudes hardened.

Into this context, a young, single woman arrived. Born into a wealthy Muslim family, Luma Mufleh was a talented soccer player in high school who left her Jordanian homeland on her own to attend Smith College in Massachusetts, and remained after graduation because she could not accept the expectations for a traditional woman in her home society. On a whim, she moved to Atlanta, where she happened upon Clarkston one day and a group of boys playing soccer in a parking lot and began to join their games. One thing led to another as she gradually became better acquainted with the boys' lives, and in due time, the Fugees were born, a program that grew into three soccer teams.

Coaching the boys enlightened Luma to their larger lives. She learned that many of them lacked basic education skills, and so she started offering after-school tutoring. She discovered that their families needed help with completing immigration documents, dealing with school personnel, making medical and social service appointments, and the like. The work she was doing soon involved making connections with the whole town. For example, she had to find a suitable soccer field and overcome local resistance from the mayor and city council. Other business people caught some of her spirit and came to see the value of employing immigrants and offering goods and services they needed.

Then Luma got directly into the education business by launching her own Fugees Academy, which now offers education to both boys and girls in grades six through twelve. It is the only school in the United States focused entirely on refugee education (Fugees Academy n.d.), and in 2018 it expanded its program to Columbus, Ohio, where its national headquarters is now located with plans for more expansion. Its year-round approach includes after-school and summer programming, and soccer remains an integral part of the Fugees' identity.

Why is this story so important? Simply because it demonstrates how one woman's remarkable dedication and vision could stimulate the transformation of a deeply divided, typical small American town that now welcomes forty nationalities speaking sixty languages (Stump 2018), with a town motto of "Small Town, Big Heart" (n.d.). And the school she founded has become a shining example of "provid[ing] comprehensive wrap-around services for students and their families" (Fugees Academy n.d.), the topic of this book.

Not all immigrants come to this country with the same challenges as these refugees, but they all encounter questions of assimilation and enculturation in a new and often very foreign land. Yet, they collectively enhance us as a nation by what they bring and create once they arrive here. On a practical, economic level, "More than forty percent of companies on the US Fortune 500 list were launched by immigrants or children of immigrants," according to Leadem (2017), a statistic that far exceeds the proportion of immigrants in this country. These entrepreneurs, in turn, create jobs for other American workers and help to build the overall economy. Their education level of attainment tends to be as high or higher than native-born citizens (Barshay 2018), and they are innovators, including many Nobel Prize winners (McCready 2017).

However, even more importantly, immigrants enrich our perspectives and help those of us who were born here to see life in new ways by "chang[ing] our angle of vision" (Wittman 2012, B7). It's not a one-way street of us helping them; we have as much to gain from our immigrants, and they are vitally important to what makes America great already. Indeed, a 2017 op-ed piece in the *New York Times* argues that more immigration would make America greater (Porter 2017).

So, who counts as "American"? We all do—native born and immigrant alike—and we need to open our doors, hearts, and minds to each other, not build walls. Let's work together to help each other succeed; it is in the best interest of us all to do so. This title addresses how to make educating immigrants a school-home-community success story.

REFERENCES

Barshay, J. 2018. "Most Immigrants Outpace Americans When It Comes to Education—With One Big Exception." *The Hechinger Report*, March 19. Retrieved from https://hechingerreport.org/most-immigrants-outpace-americans-when-it-comes-to-education-with-one-big-exception/.

Chen, M. 2016. "Undocumented Immigrants Contribute Over \$11 Billion to Our Economy Each Year." *Immigration Policy*, March 14. Retrieved from https://www.thenation.com/article/undocumented-immigrants-contribute-over-11-billion-to-our-economy-each-year/.

Current Population Survey—March 2010 Detailed Tables. 2010. Retrieved from https://www.census.gov/data/tables/2010/demo/foreign-born/cps-2010.html.

Current Population Survey—March 2016 Detailed Tables. 2016. Retrieved from https://www.census.gov/data/tables/2016/demo/foreign-born/cps-2016.html.

Estimates of the Unauthorized Immigrant Population Residing in the United States. 2018. Homeland Security. Retrieved from https://www.dhs.gov/immigration-statistics/population-estimates/unauthorized-resident.

Fugees Academy. (n.d.). Retrieved from https://www.fugeesfamily.org/about-us.

Krogstad, J. M., and J. Radford, J. 2017. *Key Facts about Refugees to the US*. Pew Research Center. Retrieved from http://www.pewresearch.org/fact-tank/2017/01/30/key-facts-about-refugees-to-the-u-s/.

Leadem, R. 2017. "The Immigrant Entrepreneurs behind Major American Companies." *Entrepreneur*, February 4. Retrieved from https://www.entrepreneur.com/article/288687.

McCready, R. (2017). "15 Charts Explaining Why Immigration Is Good for Innovation." Retrieved from https://venngage.com/blog/why-immigration-is-good/.

"On World Refugee Day, UN Urges Support, Solidarity for Record Number of Displaced People." 2017. *UN News*. Retrieved from https://news.un.org/en/story/2017/06/559872-world-refu
gee-day-un-urges-support-solidarity-record-number-displaced-people.

Porter, E. 2017. "How to Make America Greater: More Immigration." *New York Times*, February 7. Retrieved from https://www.nytimes.com/2017/02/07/business/economy/restricting-immigration-would-make-america-smaller-not-greater.html.

St. John, W. 2009. *Outcasts United: An American Town, a Refugee Team, and One Woman's Quest to Make a Difference*. New York: Spiegel and Grau.

Stump, S. 2018. "'One America': Small Town Welcomes Thousands of Refugees with Southern Hospitality." *Today*. Retrieved from https://www.today.com/news/clarkston-georgia-home-thousands-refugees-t132421.

Tan, S. 2006. *The Arrival*. New York: Arthur A. Levine.

Vargas, J. A. 2012. "We Are Americans* *Just Not Legally." *Time*, June 25, 34–44.

Wittman, J. 2012. "Hardship and Humor of the Immigrant Life: Memoirs Review." *Washington Post*, May 27, B7.

"SILENCED BY LANGUAGE"

Christina Levy

A woman mispronounces the word "can't" as "cyann."
The opening "c" sound escapes
from her abdomen as if she is choking
on a piece of bone that she sucked all the marrow
from at dinner. The rest of the word sings
its way off of her tongue and hinges midair before falling

"cyaan."

Across the room, the woman's son
who is just as immigrant as she corrects her;
*The word is can't, not "cyaan." If you are in
America, speak like an English speaking American.
If you are in Jamaica, speak like a Jamaican.*

His urgency is terrifying and insensitive
to his mother whose body I watch
instantly recoil into itself before she commands
her tongue and voice to bend—

"Can't."

The sound searches for a space to land, but
not even her voice welcomes it. I sit
and wonder how often she is forced
into this silence—one defined as being unheard,
misunderstood, and corrected.

She turns and smiles at me.
I avert my gaze, afraid that maybe her eyes
will detect some lingering stain of what I
gave America to wash from me:
the same stubborn dialect,
the same thick tongue,
the same
Jamaica.

INTRODUCTION

Immigrant Discourses beyond Educational Spaces

Ruth McKoy Lowery, Mary Ellen Oslick, and Rose M. Pringle

Immigrants and issues surrounding immigration have been prominent in major educational, political, and economic rhetoric for decades. Foner (2009) found that "the number of immigrants in the United States has risen to an all-time high" (7). However, negative sentiments surrounding issues of immigration have escalated across the United States as several states seek to curtail their immigrant population growth (Brown 2016).

Children do not make the choice to immigrate. The adults in their lives usually make this decision. Hence, these children come to the United States, sometimes against their will but mostly with the understanding that the adults have the best intentions for their immigration patterns. Because children are a major factor in the debate, it is important then to have a conversation about what issues of immigration mean to and for them. How can schools, communities, churches, and other stakeholders accommodate their needs? How can these entities create welcoming environments where these young involuntary immigrants can thrive?

The purpose of this book is to address and extend the discussion on immigration, with the hope of stimulating a greater and open dialogue among schools, immigrant families, and the communities where they live, work, and participate. Sharing examples and stories from the education and community perspectives can help preserve and in-service teachers as they work in classrooms with immigrant students. For the purposes of this book, the term "immigrant" comprises voluntary and involuntary immigrant and refugee populations.

WHY IMMIGRATION?

Many of today's immigrant groups worry about the impact current and future immigration policies will have on them and their families. Experiencing the negative effects of the current American economy and political climate, many immigrants find their achievement of a piece of the American pie quickly slipping away as they struggle to take care of their families, meet their living expenses, and ensure a quality education for their children.

A quality education is of importance for children of immigrants as they adjust to life in their newly adopted home country. Educating these children to enter the economy and society of twenty-first-century America is often a task of immense challenge (Holdaway and Alba 2009). However, Adelman and Taylor (2015) determined that the school environment, a "natural place for meeting many needs of immigrant youngsters and their families" (324), can alleviate some of these challenges.

In the last few decades, the number of immigrants have surpassed other immigrant periods. Dreby and Adkins (2010) articulated that the hallmark of this increased immigrant wave is the diversity of the group, the largest numbers arriving from countries in Asia and Latin America. This change in immigrant patterns has realized an increase in refugees, fearing persecution, war, and famine in their homelands (Adelman and Taylor 2015). Many of these sojourners are sometimes unaccompanied minors, young children traveling without safe parental guides (Linsky 2017).

IMPACT ON SCHOOLS

As the pattern of new incoming students change, teachers learn to accommodate them, while addressing the needs of all students in their classrooms. They also have to learn to communicate with families. Traditionally, there has been an accepted understanding that schools would welcome and orient newcomers, work to improve the English skills of those with limited English proficiency, and assist families with finding some neighborhood services.

Adelman and Taylor (2015) reported that according to the US Department of Education's 2015 report there are approximately 840,000 immigrant K–12 students and 4.6 million English language learners in US schools. Additionally, the number born in other countries or born in the US of immigrant parents is increasing faster than any other group (Nwosu, Batalova, and Auclair 2014). These rapid changes often result in less than positive experiences in schools as immigrant policies are interpreted differently. Hence, the need for a culturally relevant approach to address the needs of immigrant students.

According to Brown-Jeffy and Cooper (2011), a "culturally relevant pedagogy is a way for schools to acknowledge the home-community culture of the students, and through sensitivity to cultural nuances integrate these cultural experiences, values, and understandings into the teaching and learning environment" (67). It is important, then, to engage students within a model of culturally responsive teaching in classrooms.

Teachers become culturally relevant when they acknowledge and accept the experiences of their students. They ensure that all students feel welcomed in their classrooms, regardless of their cultural, racial, or ethnic backgrounds. Immigrant students are able to flourish in diverse, yet welcoming classrooms when culturally responsive pedagogy is employed.

IMPACT ON HOMES AND COMMUNITIES

Many of the current immigrant student population do not have English as their first language. This sometimes causes problems, as parents are unaware of the resources available to them and their children. Many parents depend on their children to communicate with schools and services in their communities, but this can be problematic. Landale, Thomas, and Van Hook (2011) argued that immigrant children's living arrangement is important because this is where they receive the most help. How do communities try to help them to acclimate to the new home and environments?

Community groups provide some services to help immigrant families, often meeting their basic needs for food, clothing, and shelter. Establishing a sense of community also includes supporting immigrant families' success and focusing on hope for the future. These goals can be attempted with several simple, but impactful measures. One course of action is enhancing the use of volunteers and other community resources to support immigrant families. Additionally, increasing the range of options and choices for students can be achieved by weaving together school and community efforts.

Landale et al. (2011) posited that immigrant children's "health and development, educational attainment, and future social and economic integration will play a defining role in the nation's future" (64). It is paramount then to create a positive connection among schools, homes, and community that calls for open communication.

OVERVIEW OF THE BOOK

There are ten chapters in this book, excluding the introduction. The chapters offer different perspectives on immigrant children and families in the United States and end with a series of questions to guide the reflection of the readings. The chapters are further divided into three sections: a research and implementation strand, a practice and reflection strand, and a resources strand. Additionally, the book opens with a poem and ends with a comprehensive sample of resources for those working with or wanting to learn more about immigrant populations.

Section I takes a more theoretical look at the issues surrounding various immigrant groups. In chapter 1, authors Lowery and Pringle discuss the experiences of Jamaican immigrant parents and their experiences with their children's schooling experiences. In chapter 2, author Ogodo describes experiences of Nigerian college graduates when they immigrate to the United States. Chapter 3 by Subedi, Maleku, and Pyakurel describe the experiences of Bhutanese-Nepali women and their adjustment to a new living experience in the United States. In chapter 4, Winterbottom shares experiences of Japanese immigrant mothers and discusses how teachers can help them to navigate the education with their young children. Finally, in chapter 5, Sivashankar shares how dramatic inquiry and a children's picture book can be used to help preservice teachers dialogue about immigration issues.

Section II presents stories of educators and community leaders, the work they do with immigrant students and their families and some first-hand experiences of immigrant students and families. In chapter 6, Moore and Darby share the intense work they do through Usher's New Look, a program instituted in several states to help transform immigrant teens' experiences in the United States. Chapter 7 by Geiger is told from a principal's perspective. Geiger presents a narrative of a student displaced by Hurricane Maria and shares how the school community worked to help him feel at home. In chapter 8, Benain-Reid-McKoy discusses her early experiences as an immigrant student and then shares how she uses her expertise as a financial advisor to help immigrant families with positive financial literacy. Finally, in the last chapter in this section, chapter 9, McDonald describes how she transformed her personal tragedy and experience into advocacy for at-risk and displaced individuals.

Section III ends with chapter 10, by Oslick, Goins, and Brown, presenting a comprehensive description of resources that can help immigrant students, their families, and other stakeholders interested in working with immigrant populations. Overall, the works included in this volume are intended to foster further dialogue about immigration and its impact on the home, school, and community.

Immigration is a family, community, and school issue. It is imperative that we all engage in conversations about what issues of immigration mean to children and what these issues mean for them. What can schools do to accommodate their needs? What can the community do to accommodate their needs? How can their home environment affect their well-being? This book is a guide to issues that address and extend the discussion on these questions.

In sum, the authors address current issues of immigration across a wide spectrum, and identify best practices for engaging immigrant families, educators, and community members in a successful and hopeful future in the United States. Our hope is that reading these perspectives will help create a more open dialogue among schools, families, and their communities.

REFERENCES

Adelman, H. S., and L. Taylor. 2015. "Immigrant Children and Youth in the USA: Facilitating Equity of Opportunity at School." *Education Sciences* 5 (4): 323–44.

Brown, J. A. 2016. "Running on Fear: Immigration, Race and Crime Framings in Contemporary GOP Presidential Debate Discourse." *Critical Criminology* 24 (3): 315–31.

Brown-Jeffy, S., and J. E. Cooper. 2011. "Toward a Conceptual Framework of Culturally Relevant Pedagogy: An Overview of the Conceptual and Theoretical Literature." *Teacher Education Quarterly* 38 (1): 65–84.

Dreby, J., and T. Adkins. 2010. "Inequalities in Transnational Families." *Sociology Compass* 4 (8): 673–89.

Foner, N. 2009. "The American Melting Pot Is a Rich Stew." *Phi Kappa Phi Forum* 89 (2): 7–10.

Holdaway, J., and R. Alba. 2009. "Educating Immigrant Youth: The Role of Institutions and Agency." *Teachers College Record* 111 (3): 597–615.

Landale, N. S., K. J. A. Thomas, and J. Van Hook. 2011. "The Living Arrangements of Children of Immigrants." *The Future of Children* 21 (1): 43–70.

Linsky, M. 2017. "Immigrant Children at Risk." *Georgia Bar Journal* 22 (6): 28–34.

Nwosu, C., J. Batalova, and G. Auclair. 2014. *Frequently Requested Statistics on Immigrants and Immigration in the United States*. Washington, DC: Migration Policy Institute.

Section I

Research and Implementation

1

OUR STORIES

Voices of Jamaican Immigrant Parents

Ruth McKoy Lowery and Rose M. Pringle

You don't seem to understand my predicament. I have to work to support these kids. I don't have time nor money to go back to school. I can barely make it from one day to the next.
—Kevin

When I look back on my teaching job in Jamaica, and where I was in life, it's hard to think I traded all of this for the dream of making it better in America. I have never worked so hard in my life and yet I am hardly making it. It's hard but still I hope my children will be the better for all the sacrifices we make for them.
—Jasmine

In ongoing discussions with Jamaican immigrant parents and their experiences adapting to the education system in the United States, the opening epigraphs represent persistent views. Many Jamaicans, like other immigrant groups, have settled in major urban cities in the United States (Awokoya and Clark 2008). However, many still have strong ties to their families back in their homeland (Forsythe-Brown et al. 2017).

Often constructed as privileged among other black immigrants, Jamaicans are viewed as having the opportunity for advancement (Hines 1997). However, the varying continuum that differentiates the socioeconomic levels of many Jamaican immigrants is often ignored. Jamaicans, like other West Indians immigrating to the United States, come from a variety of socioeconomic backgrounds (Kirkwood 2000). Many, having already established levels of economic independence in their homeland, have had to leave Jamaica in search of a better future.

Eroding salaries and declining living standards in the last decades have provoked a mass exodus of all social classes in search of a better life in the United States (Ho 1999). Foner (1987) further determined that a variety of social, economic, and political factors in Jamaica explain the recent mass immigration to the United States. This large-scale movement from Jamaica is rooted in the harsh realities of the Jamaican economy. The diminishing economy and reduced opportunities for advancement in decreasing industries have resulted in many immigrant families' inability to maintain a decent lifestyle and to secure an adequate educational future for their children on the island.

In a longitudinal study conducted with predominant Jamaican immigrant parents living in the southern United States, the authors of this chapter recorded individual, small-, and large-group conversations with parents. After consenting with the parents, the researchers selected four parents for more in-depth individual interviews. The second author conducted a final set of interviews with the parents to glean a deeper understanding of their experiences.

Using the constant comparative method of qualitative analysis (Maykut and Morehouse 1999), initial codes and identification of data relevant to immigrant parent experiences occurred as both researchers listened to the recordings. These codes were then used as the starting point for continued data analysis of the formal interviews with the four participants. More focused coding resulted in elimination and/or combination of codes that were then organized into themes grounded in literature related to issues of immigrants and culturally responsive pedagogy.

The four participants were strategically selected because of the positions they occupied within Jamaica's educational system and their consistent articulation of their beliefs about the transformative role of education in social and economic mobility. More so, over the two-year period the researchers observed their frustration as they tried to understand and navigate the school system. These parents, quite notably, never wavered in their enthusiasm that their children would be successful.

Pseudonyms are used to represent each of the parents as we tell their stories. In the remainder of this chapter, we focus on the experiences of these four Jamaican immigrant parents and their efforts to navigate and situate their children in the American education system. Although they find it difficult to pursue their own education in their present circumstances, these parents hope for a good education for their children—the seminal reason many immigrate.

A major concern is their worry about the negative stereotype often placed on them about their lack of involvement with their children's day-to-day schooling experience (Mitchell and Bryan 2007). The goal of sharing these parents' stories is to continue the dialogue toward bridging the school-home-community gap so that school personnel will understand the specific needs of this population toward promoting culturally relevant learning environments.

IMMIGRANT PARENTS: REASONS THEY COME

Research indicates that better economic situations and educational opportunities for their children are the primary reasons for immigration (Suárez-Orozco, Suárez-Orozco, and Todorova 2008). They depart Jamaica self-confidently with a will to ascend socially and achieve economically but often find themselves blocked along the way for reasons that have nothing to do with the merit and work ethic they value so highly (Vickerman 1999). However, with this new environment comes new frustration, as the initial acclimation period can be very traumatic.

Some immigrants end up living with extended relatives who offer promise of a better life, while also resorting to jobs well below their ability to make a decent living. Many who were able to command a certain level of financial independence and respect in their homeland quickly realize that their education level is not a guarantee for immediate equitable employment to continue their familiar lifestyle (Shodavaram et al. 2009). Arriving with the desire to continue in their jobs, Rhone (2007) noted that these immigrants soon realize that they have to pursue additional education for jobs for which they already have years of experience in their country.

Because of the social and economic adjustments, many Jamaican immigrant parents find themselves unable to provide the necessary support for their children who are navigating the American educational system. Profiling the experiences of immigrant parents who were educators in their country and for whom immigration portended social and economic mobility funneled by education, is one way of sharing how important it is to understand the family and community for the children in school spaces.

Jasmine's Story:

Jasmine, one of the parents quoted in the opening epigraph was a secondary [high school] English teacher in Jamaica. Several years ago, she immigrated, and now finds herself working two and sometimes three jobs to support her family here in the United States, and in addition, sends money home to support her extended family back in Jamaica. As a voluntary immigrant (Ogbu 1991), Jasmine constantly compares the socioeconomic and political situation in the United States to those in Jamaica. She, however, notes, "it is hard here but there is hope for me and my two children." Expressing a confidence in America's education system, she further illuminates that possibilities are endless for her children to excel in America.

Jasmine embraces the notion that education positions one for upward social and economic mobility, a sentiment that exists in Jamaica and is regularly espoused by their educators and politicians. In addition, she sees education as critical to the transformation of her socioeconomic well-being as indicated in the goals she articulated for herself. She says, "One day I will go back to school and get an American degree but that will be after my children are secured in their education."

Despite the discomfort with her job and the financial setback, Jasmine interprets her life at this time as being one of much sacrifice for the well-being of her children. She acknowledges the difficulty the children are experiencing at school but declares her hopefulness in their success because of the range of opportunities she sees existing from public schools through to college. Some of the difficulties she describes as being due to the language barrier and expresses that her children, like many before them, will overcome and will eventually speak like Americans. Jasmine explains, "Children pick up the American accent easier than us adults and as soon as they cross that bridge I am confident that they will do well in school."

Melvie's Story:

Melvie describes herself as a former civil servant in the Jamaican education system. For over ten years, she was an officer with responsibility for primary school education. However, as the country's economic system declined and political violence increased, she decided to immigrate with her husband and three daughters to the United States. Before immigrating, her youngest daughter (Janie), at age eleven, a high achiever in the Jamaican education system, was successful in the national examination and was awarded a scholarship to one of the prestigious high schools noted for academic excellence.

Upon arrival in the United States, Janie entered tenth grade in an urban high school. She was initially placed in the lowest track and immediately recognized that she was with kids who were not expected to enter college. As a result of her placement, she was not offered college prep courses. Melvie advocated for her daughter and the school moved her into higher-level courses after seeing how well she did in her classes. "I cannot believe they did that to my daughter," Melvie shared as she thought about how promising her daughter was in the Jamaican education system. "Why do you think they did that?" she asked, and immediately said, "I wanted to send all of them back so badly especially when the teacher told me my daughter was not speaking well, but my mother is now old and is unable to look after all three of them. If I had the money, I would send the youngest one to private school because she is so bright [smart] and I know she will do well."

Currently, Janie is preparing for the SAT and is involved in self-study to attain a score that can possibly get her a scholarship. While Melvie is secure in her daughters' abilities, there is still the concern of costs of college for her two older children. She further laments that such concern was defying one of the main reason why she made the decision to immigrate "to secure a safe and educative future for my daughters."

Her two older daughters, enrolled in the local community college, are working to contribute to the family's welfare and fund themselves through their college program. "If we were back home, things would be different." Alluding to social unrests, Melvie explained, "I would have the financial security but probably at the cost of a brighter future for my girls, especially my youngest. More so, there are so many opportunities here from which my girls can choose and that would be a fulfillment of my dreams."

In preparation for immigration, Melvie did some research on colleges and had conversations with her girls about their possible career choices. Her findings confirmed her beliefs that America would offer many more opportunities for them than what was offered or available in her own country, Jamaica.

Kevin's Story:

Kevin, a high school accountant from Jamaica, now works as a technician in a major hospital in the southern end of the state. Kevin knows the culture of schools from a Jamaican perspective, having spent nearly twenty years managing the school's budget in liaison with the financial officer from the ministry of education [Department of Education]. His impetus to immigrate was funneled by family encouragement, the hope of a better life, and his mother's commitment to provide them the choice of relocating to the United States.

After waiting nearly ten years for an immigrant visa filed by his mother, Kevin and his siblings were approved and, they, along with their families, all immigrated to the United States. As a believer in education and its role in deciding their economic well-being, Kevin is concerned about his four children and the extent to which they will be successful in this new education system. His concerns have arisen because of the number of times he has been called to the school for "minor infractions."

Kevin expresses that teachers in Jamaica from early childhood to high school often take an active role in disciplining students and orienting them toward schoolwork. His experiences over the last four years as an immigrant parent are that in the American system, teachers rely solely on parents to be disciplinarians. "I expect the teacher to be in charge of school stuff. Not that I should not go in, but what is the point of my visiting the school every day? What does that say to my child? That they cannot manage him."

According to Kevin each time he has to take time off from his work to visit his children's school impacts his ability to provide for his family. He further explains, "I wouldn't be so concerned if I was seeing progress, but each time I am more certain they think my children cannot talk the American language, are losers, and do not have any hope of succeeding."

In one of his more passionate moments, Kevin says, "I have news for them. I have news for them. My children are going to make a better life for themselves in this very same system."

Carmen's Story:

Carmen was a Home Economics teacher in a non-traditional [technical] high school in Jamaica. She was noted for her culinary skills and constantly reminisces about the number of awards she received during her tenure. Faced with the opportunity for immigration, Carmen expressed that this was an easy choice. A single parent of three, Carmen thought that immigrating to the United States would be advantageous to her and her children.

Her culinary skills would make her marketable and she would be able to guarantee her children's success in schools. "I have always guided my children in their schoolwork and they have always been at the top of their classes." After five years, Carmen is still struggling to realize her American dreams. Her jobs with the food industry have been sporadic, and attempts to start her own business have been severely hampered due to insufficient collateral to procure business loans. At the same time, two of her children are struggling through middle and high school.

Carmen now has the dubious task of negotiating her way through the American school system as she seeks to affirm her children's positive schooling experiences. At a recent parent-teacher conference, Carmen was surprised and literally embarrassed, as she was made aware of her children's poor academic performance, inability to express themselves in English, and their less than acceptable behavior patterns as described by the teachers.

Having spoken to the teachers, Carmen lamented that her children were having difficulty adjusting to the more liberal and democratic atmosphere in the American schools. Even more surprising to her is the notion that her children were being labeled as deficient in both written and oral communication skills. She expressed dissatisfaction that most of the teachers complained about the accent of the children and the need for them to become understandable.

While Carmen is very concerned about the children's academic performance and the impact of the Jamaican accent on their abilities to communicate with their teachers, she is very unhappy with the disciplinary issues that have arisen. One of her two high school children is in regular education tracking courses and for the last two years has consistently performed below his mother's expectation as she demands more of him academically. "I do not want him labeled and I know where this is going," Carmen declares. When asked to explain, Carmen noted that "poor performance and bad behavior do not lead to any kind of stability or acceptable life." In a tone of defiance she further explains, "I do not want them as adults to be dependent on the state or me. I do not want that! They are here to make good use of the educational opportunities and by gosh, they will."

FINDINGS AND DISCUSSION

One of our goals as Jamaican immigrants who have successfully navigated America's educational system is to underscore the importance of dialogue between the school system and the parents of Jamaican immigrant children. Research indicates that many immigrants have come to this country embracing education and their children's schooling experiences as the vehicle for socioeconomic mobility (Kirkwood 2000).

In the process, we profile Jamaican immigrant parents who as educators from their country have articulated the importance of education for their children's well-being but are hampered by sociopolitical realities of their newly adopted country. In conducting the research, we identified recurring themes as they emerged during the biannual seminar that included presentation on understanding America's education system and college access. The seminar included formal presentations, informal discussions and a range of informal interviews. We then conducted formal interviews with the parents whose stories are told above.

These parents' expressions of their experiences are reflective of the stories commonly told to us by Jamaican immigrant parents. As we further deliberate their stories, two major themes ascertained from our discussions are: "frustrations of Jamaican immigrant parents" and "barriers and disconnect at the seam between Jamaican immigrant home culture and the school culture."

Frustrations of Jamaican Immigrant Parents

Many Jamaicans leave their country self-confidently imbued with a will to ascend socially and achieve academically but often find themselves blocked along the way for reasons that have nothing to do with the merit and work ethic they value so highly (Rhone 2007). They leave an environment that places much value on the transformative role of education and the benefits of good schooling experiences.

This belief about the role of education as a means for socioeconomic mobility is also the foundation for frustration among Jamaican immigrant parents who were involved in education in their home country. These parents brought a level of awareness in general about the role of education and constantly expressed a strong desire for upward mobility for their children and also for themselves. This awareness is grounded in their belief system and becomes "hope" for their children's success attainable via a good education system.

Despite the issues that have arisen for their children at school and the negative trajectory toward economic stability, this awareness becomes their hope. All four parents expressed such awareness and hope. This hope, however, is not translated into immediate reality due to the "disconnect" between Jamaican immigrant parents and the school system. While many of the immigrant parents have awareness of their Jamaican educational system from being educated in pre-kindergarten to post-secondary, they lack knowledge of the complex nature and the savvy of navigating the American educational system for their children.

It was clear that all four parents immigrated with the desire to support their children's academic success and their own personal desires to continue in their chosen fields. They quickly realized the hurdles to their upward social and economic mobility; however, it is often difficult for them to grasp this reality. Jasmine, Melvie, Kevin, and Carmen are all currently employed outside the American educational system. They will have to update their degrees and/or teaching certificates before they can be eligible to teach in American classrooms.

Availability of funds is a constant source of frustration for these parents as they find it very costly to update their education credentials here in the United States. They cannot see themselves updating their teaching credentials in the near future because they have to work to provide for their immediate families. According to Jasmine, "Just to have my degree validated and compared to the American certification, the lawyer was charging over one hundred dollars. I just could not afford it at the time, so here I am busting myself [working hard] at two jobs." Still, Jasmine laments that she wants to return to school and is currently saving. However, she is changing to the health profession whereas she says, "In two years part time I can be an RN [registered nurse]. So I can work and gain experience in my current job, go to college, and increase my earning power at the end of the two years." Her concerns are that in the meantime, "My kids are going to be left at the mercy of the school system."

Many of the parents cannot afford the funds needed to return to school and the hours needed to focus on education classes, work, and supporting their families seem impossible. Thus, they see the continuation of a career they succeeded at before slowly slipping away as the years go by. For them, the current realities of their parental responsibilities are more important in their present circumstances. Hence, like Jasmine, they gravitate toward another career, usually one that is aligned with their current employment.

The parents expressed their sadness that the issue of race is so often and quickly raised in discussions about their jobs, experiences, and effectiveness as workers in the larger work force. Kevin noted that race was not an important factor in Jamaica. "If you have the skills, you will get the job. Here, I realize, that even with the skills, you sometimes can't get a good job, so I have to take what I can until I can sort myself out." Although issues of race and class have shaped Jamaica's society, these topics according to Rhone (2007) are not the focal point of discussion when dealing with matters, including those related to education. However, these concerns become front and center in one's existence, and especially for Jamaican immigrants navigating their way in this new society.

These parents realize the importance of education for their children and are determined that their children should not experience the same problems in the future. Each expresses that their educational attainment is placed on hold so they can provide for their children. Kevin and Carmen were vociferous in their pronouncement that their children will learn and will be successful. Thus, despite their personal frustrations, these parents have high hopes for their children's futures. They are determined that against all odds they, and their children, will be successful in this country and educational system.

Barriers and Disconnect at the Seam:
Home versus School Cultures

Many Jamaican parents aspire toward higher educational advancement for their children. They realize that in order to acquire respectable jobs and to gain stability, their children need to effectively negotiate the American education system. Many Jamaican-born immigrant children arrive in America with a sound knowledge base and social skills, and can compete successfully (Kirkwood 2000). This factor is sometimes not acknowledged as there is often a "disconnect" at the seam between the Jamaican home culture and the existing American school culture.

Parents often lament that the schools sometimes do not have their children's best interest at heart and that the children are often labeled simply because of their "Jamaican accent." Janie's experience was indicative of this quick-to-judge mentality that school officials often institute when deciding immigrant children's placement in classes. They were unaware of her level of achievement and seemingly made academic decisions for Janie without consulting her prior school records and talking with her parents.

Immigrant parents like Jasmine, who are concerned about education, are determined to have their children excel in the American school system. They realize that the strong emphasis placed on educational achievement in the Jamaican system is even more important, and a direct route for social mobility, in the United States. Thus, Jasmine, Melvie, Kevin, and Carmen have transferred this high value for education to the United States as they seek to increase the educational outcomes for their children toward future successful careers. They work extra jobs to attain an adequate lifestyle and to be able to live where their children can attend "good schools." They are disappointed at the negative labels placed on them because they are not more involved with the school and education community.

In Jamaica when the children arrive at school, they are the responsibilities of the teacher. Teachers are sometimes told by parents to do whatever it takes for learning to occur. Parents are expected to offer support to school such as ensuring that the children appear clean at school and are provided with the materials and supplies needed for learning. Parents generally admonish their children to be respectful to teachers, and the schools usually handle discipline problems for both minor and major offenses.

In American schools, however, parents like Kevin quickly realize that this mode of operation is not accepted. Like Kevin, the other parents express concerns that teachers would call them for "simple offenses" such as talking out of turn in class and not turning in homework on time. Jasmine shared, "Those were things I nipped in the bud in my classroom. Students knew from day one what I would and would not accept in my class and they knew they would be punished immediately. I can't see calling parents with minor things like that. Teachers should be trained to handle that."

Because of often stringent work schedules, parents are unable to visit schools and to keep up with the welfare of their children's performance. Thus, they are perceived as poor parents, uncaring of the welfare of their children. This lack of cultural understanding between the school and home often results in a tension between parents and school personnel. The schools value the parent involvement that includes school visits, but parents' non-involvement often conveys the wrong message, that they do not care.

Often when the parents do have to attend meetings with the school, they share that they experience hostility from school personnel. Kevin shared that he "straightened out his son," laying down the law on what he expected from him. He also talked with the teacher, asked her to be more assertive in talking with him, and assured her that he would be "staying on top of things at home." "He is here to learn, not to play around," Kevin asserted.

All four parents shared concerns about other immigrant parents who are unfamiliar with the education system here. Carmen voiced, "If we have it so hard and we know about higher education, what will parents who have no clue do?" Kevin affirmed that now he is familiar with how "minor offenses" can derail his son's education, he is determined to "stay on top of things" and he encourages other parents to do the same. Melvie shared that she made it a "point of duty" to find out what was expected from the school for her children.

Jasmine lamented that schools should make a greater effort to help immigrant children to succeed. "I know it is difficult, but I taught in a system where I sometimes had fifty children or more in one class. I HAD to teach them." She acknowledged that she thinks a lot of the "misunderstandings occur because they don't know us. They see parents working two and three jobs and they immediately think we're greedy. They don't realize that many of us are supporting more than one household. Some of us have to take care of our parents and other children back home. There is no welfare or social security system [in Jamaica]."

Jasmine, Melvie, Kevin, and Carmen all acknowledge that, yes, they bear some responsibility in helping school personnel better understand their experiences, cultures, and mores. While immigrant parents' initial actions with schools are constrained by their beliefs about and the expectations of schooling in America, educators contend that a considerable part of the explanation of why immigrant children struggle in schools lies in the socioeconomic inequalities and racial disparities woven into the fabric of American society (Holdaway and Alba 2009). Key players in education who are interested in creating a more open dialogue that will benefit the school-home-community must seek to provide the needed resources. All groups are responsible for educating young children who will be productive citizens in a global society.

CONCLUSION

The current wave of immigration has led to an increasingly diverse school population and has created new sets of problems. As children from so many diverse backgrounds enter the education system, many schools are inadequately prepared to serve their needs. America's welfare will be dependent on the extent to which public schools are able to educate these immigrant children (Myers 2007).

Today's immigrants represent a range of individuals, some who are skilled and educated, and others who are eager to develop skills and learn about quickly advancing technologies. There is a great need in schools for education that is high quality, multicultural, and takes into account language differences and students' diverse backgrounds.

There is an even greater need for better cultural understanding and teachers who are culturally responsive (Gay 2000). Teachers who are able to use "the cultural knowledge, prior experiences, frames of reference, and performance styles of ethnically diverse students to make learning encounters more relevant to and effective for them" (29). These teachers must treat the culture, heritage, and language of all their students with respect in order to be effective.

Further, teachers must employ an equity pedagogy which Banks and Banks (1995) articulate as "Teaching strategies and classroom environments that help students from diverse racial, ethnic, and cultural groups attain the knowledge, skills, and attitudes needed to function effectively within, and help create and perpetuate, a just, humane, and democratic society" (152).

In conversations with Jamaican parents, the authors learned a lot that now helps to shape our preparation of preservice teachers and the work we do in schools with practicing teachers. Expanding the school-home-community dialogue is feasible and creates a more meaningful universe if parents, students, teachers, and other important stakeholders are involved. To better meet the needs of all students, schools must begin by understanding and respecting the needs of their parents.

Teacher preparation programs and school community can nurture diversity by ensuring that they prepare their students and teachers in a culturally responsive environment. They have to ensure that preservice teachers see beyond current media representations. Universities must further ensure that courses are rigorous and offer diverse perspectives. Midobuche (1999) argued that schools must also take a strong position in requiring that their teachers not only be knowledgeable about issues of diversity, but also actually incorporate these concepts into their teaching and daily interactions with all students.

Schools need to create an open environment where parents feel welcomed and where they understand that teachers and others involved will help them to actualize their educational vision for their children. Schools have to play a more active role in the immigrant community by being more visible to parents and students and creating a "safe space" for parents to feel more welcome.

The changing economy, the international unrests, the dream of upward social mobility and many other factors still hold true for many immigrant families who make their way to the United States each year. Ensuring that parents' voices are heard in the school-home-community dialogue will strengthen the educational development of their children as we reinforce that all children can learn and can be successful in school.

The experiences of the four parents, Jasmine, Melvie, Kevin, and Carmen, highlight this importance. The Jamaican national motto, "Out of many, one people," holds credence in the American immigrant experience today. Schools, homes, and communities must join forces as one entity so that they can provide one united front, the connecting bridge in educating all students for a brighter tomorrow.

QUESTIONS TO GUIDE DISCUSSION OF IMMIGRANT PARENTS

1. How can I make my classroom/school environment welcoming to immigrant parents and their children?
2. In what ways can I encourage immigrant parents to become participating members of the school community?
3. What strategies can I implement in my classroom so all students feel supported in taking risks as they expand their learning?
4. What services can schools collaborating with community organizations offer to immigrant students and their families?

REFERENCES

Awokoya, J. T., and C. Clark. 2008. "Demystifying Cultural Theories and Practices: Locating Black Immigrant Experiences in Teacher Education Research." *Multicultural Education* 16 (2): 49–58.

Banks, C. A. M., and J. A. Banks. 1995. "Equity Pedagogy: An Essential Component of Multicultural Education." *Theory into Practice* 34 (3): 152–58.

Foner, N. 1987. "The Jamaicans: Race and Ethnicity among Migrants in New York City." In *New Immigrants in New York*, edited by N. Foner, 195–217. New York: Columbia University Press.

Forsythe-Brown, I., R. J. Taylor, L. M. Chatters, I. O. Govia, N. Matusko, and J. S. Jackson. 2017. "Kinship Support in Jamaican Families in the USA and Jamaica." *Journal of African American Studies* 21 (2): 187–202.

Gay, G. 2000. *Culturally Responsive Teaching: Theory, Research and Practice*. New York: Teachers College Press.

Hines, D. 1997. "The Acculturation of Jamaican Children in the American Educational System." East Lansing, MI: National Center for Research on Teacher Learning (No. ED415976).

Ho, C. G. 1999. "Caribbean Transnationalism as a Gendered Process." *Latin American Perspectives* 26 (5): 34–54.

Holdaway, J., and R. Alba. 2009. "Educating Immigrant Youth: The Role of Institutions and Agency." *Teachers College Record* 111 (3): 597–615.

Kirkwood, T. F. 2000. "The Marginalization of Jamaican Immigrants of Color in the United States: An Interview." *Social Education* 64 (2): 94–96.

Maykut, P. S., and R. Morehouse. 1999. *Beginning Qualitative Research: A Philosophic and Practical Guide*. London: Falmer Press.

Midobuche, E. 1999. "Respect in the Classroom: Reflections of a Mexican-American Educator." *Educational Leadership* 56 (7): 80–82.

Mitchell, N. A., and J. A. Bryan. 2007. "School-Family-Community Partnerships: Strategies for School Counselors Working with Caribbean Immigrant Families." *Professional School Counseling* 10 (4): 399–409.

Myers, D. 2007. *Immigrants and Boomers: Forging a New Social Contract for the Future of America.* New York: Russell Sage Foundation.

Ogbu, J. U. (1991). "Immigration and Involuntary Minorities in Comparative Perspective." In *Minority Status and Schooling: A Comparative Study of Immigrant and Involuntary Minorities*, edited by M. A. Gibson and J. U. Ogbu, 3–33. Ithaca, NY: Cornell University.

Rhone, A. 2007. "Caribbean-Immigrant Educators: More Than an Ocean of Difference." *Childhood Education* 84 (1): 44–47.

Shodavaram, M. P., L. A. Jones, L. R. Weaver, J. A. Márquez, and A. L. Ensle. 2009. "Education of Non-European Ancestry Immigrant Students in Suburban High Schools." *Multicultural Education* 16 (3): 29–36.

Suárez-Orozco, C., M. M. Suárez-Orozco, and I. Todorova. 2008. *Learning a New Land: Immigrant Students in American Society.* Cambridge, MA: Harvard University Press.

Vickerman, M. 1999. "Representing West Indians in Film: Ciphers, Coons, and Criminals." *Western Journal of Black Studies* 23 (2): 83–96.

2

THE INTERSECTION OF CULTURE, SCHOLARSHIP, AND SURVIVAL

Nigerian College Graduates in America's Higher Institutions

Justina Ogodo

Since the passing of the US Immigration Act of 1990 and other legislation, there has been an increasing number of college-educated individuals migrating into the United States from developing countries especially from the continent of Africa (Migration Policy Institute [MPI] 2014). The exodus from Africa is often propelled by the crisis of unemployment, sociocultural insecurity, and inequalities coupled with the socioeconomic milieu of the continent, which has created frustration for families (Adepoju 2008). The issue of immigration in America continues to be controversial and the increasingly heated debate has led to many contentious issues.

The National Academies of Sciences, Engineering, and Medicine (NASEM 2015) indicates that most issues on immigration debate are based on information that is mostly misrepresented or not represented in a way that informs the public. The report, *The Integration of Immigrants into American Society*, contradicts many of the misperceptions about immigrants currently being circulated. It showed that immigrants to the United States have comparable levels of education to native-born Americans.

A New American Economy (NAE 2018) report indicates that "African immigrants attain higher levels of education than the overall US population as a whole" (9) and that the degrees earned by this category of immigrants are often in a science, technology, engineering, and mathematics, or STEM, field. In 2015, it was reported that 40 percent of African immigrants held a bachelor's degree or higher, compared to the US-born at 30.9 percent, and overall immigrant population at 29.7 percent (MPI 2014; NAE 2018). Fu (2017) also stated that despite the narrative that uneducated and unskilled immigrants enter the United States to dominate job markets, the data tell a different story.

According to the U.S. Census Bureau (2008–2012), Nigerians were shown to have the most educated group of immigrants in the country. The report indicated that 37 percent of Nigerian immigrants had a bachelor's degree, 17 percent had master's degrees, and about 4 percent had a doctorate. Since that 2006 report, the number of Nigerians with advanced degrees has grown to 29 percent (MPI 2014). Similarly, a World Bank Development Prospects Group (2007) reported that of all migrants into the United States, 60.5 percent of Nigerians had bachelor's degrees or higher. Regardless of which side of the debate spectrum one belongs, it is expedient to consider some basic facts in order to make informed judgments.

The emigration of well-educated professionals and skilled workers from developing countries threaten the economic and political development of those countries because it is the best and the brightest who move to the Western world (Ngoma and Ismail 2013). Nesbitt (2002) notes that academic exiles result from migrants who are likely to be victims of government repression even before leaving their home countries. Portes and Rumbaut (2006) agree that the majority of the migrants leave to seek economic security, educational opportunities, and better living conditions that are not readily available in their home country.

This study examined the cultural and educational influences that shaped the Nigerian college graduates through the narrative of their lived experiences. The study examined participants' a) cultural perspective and the quest for education, b) acculturation and culturally responsive teaching in America's higher education, and c) survival mechanisms employed as they pursued their dreams toward a better future. The findings may enlighten the ongoing discussions on skilled workers and educated migrants. This study is quintessential because of the current discourse on immigrants from non-White countries and issues of skilled and educated immigrants into the United States.

FROM EMIGRANTS TO IMMIGRANTS

As a major building block of any nation, Porter (1990) notes that education "increasingly constitutes the foundation of a country's competitive advantage" (260). The economic growth of a country is dependent largely on the knowledge level of its citizens. Education serves as a means of refining the life of an individual with the goal of making them better. Education makes the process of adjustment to social life more efficient as individuals progress in their experiences through life.

Education in Africa

In general, education in Africa is believed to be a key factor in the development of the individual, and in encouraging societal growth. Because of the general perception of education as a privilege and not a right, even unlearned parents struggle to ensure that their children attain some level of education, in spite of the multiple challenges faced by students and their impoverished parents.

Ijaiya (2007) posits that education in Africa serves multiple purposes of "developing the individual to the fullest of his abilities and aptitudes" as well as equipping the citizens to fully "contribute to the social and economic life of his nation and to the economic stability of oneself" (55). A blend of these two objectives ensures that the individual becomes an "asset to his community and nation" (55). Okon, Udofia, Udofia, and Udofia (2007) note that university education is an important advancement tool for citizens of African countries.

Education in Nigeria

Education is a core value of the Nigerian culture. Knowledge to a Nigerian parent is the most important factor for personal and economic development. Despite the overwhelming challenges entrenched in a culture characterized by economic inequality, poverty, and social injustice, the Nigerian parent strives to ensure their children have the opportunity to be educated. It is the single most valued legacy and inheritance parents can bestow on their children. Because of these reasons, and the society's emphasis on mandatory education, Nigerians have more post-graduate degrees than any other racial or ethnic groups (Yaqub 2007). The number

of graduates produced each year from undergraduate degrees to postgrad-
uate programs continues to rise. There are more graduates in Nigeria than
there are jobs or vocations where college-educated expertise can be utilized (Adepoju 2008). The lack of jobs leads to frustration by the graduates as well as their families. In order to survive, these graduates seek
better opportunities outside the country where they can realize their
dreams.

Emigration

Nigeria deals with emigration issues just like most developing countries
with an estimated emigration rate of 36 percent. The Organization for
Economic Cooperation and Development (OECD) notes that next to Tai-
wan, Nigeria has the second-highest percentage of highly skilled expatri-
ates in OECD countries (Dumont and Lemaître 2005). The UN Economic
Commission for Africa (UNECO) and the International Organization for
Migration (IOM) found that over 300,000 professionals reside outside
Africa, and over 30,000 of them have a doctorate.

The United Nations Development Program (UNDP 2010) estimate of
Nigerians living in other parts of the world away from home is about 1.13
million. It was also estimated that Nigerians living in the United States
will constitute 13.1 percent of the total emigrants from Africa (Development Research Centre [DRC], Global Migrant Origin Database 2007).
For physicians and nurses, the rates were about 13.6 percent and 11.7
percent, respectively.

Statistics from the US Department of Homeland Security's 2016 *Year-
book of Immigration Statistics* show that about 129,675 Nigerians obtained lawful permanent resident status in the United States between 2005
and 2014, with an average of about 13,000 every year. This trend is
expected to continue, according to the US Census Bureau, as the growing
gap in wages, living standards, and demographic features continue to
increase, and poverty, unemployment, and political instability continue to
ravage these fragile economies in developing countries (World Bank
2011). As they continue to face unemployment, emigration is the central
coping mechanism to secure their survival and that of their families.

Family Expectations and Survival Mechanism

The sociocultural characteristics of Nigeria create the quest for education by its citizens. There are high expectations placed on children to be educated based on the belief that upon graduation from college, the children can provide for themselves and their families. The burden falls on the children because education for an individual is often a communal effort. Figuratively and literally, it sometimes takes a village to train a child in Nigeria. Families often acquire enormous amounts of debt and goodwill from other family members to educate their children.

These debts and other forms of assistance are expected to be paid back or reciprocated as the graduate gets situated with a job. Economically, for over two decades, Nigeria continues to be ill-structured to meet the rising number of graduates in the country (Yaqub 2007). The lack of jobs often leads to frustration for the graduates as well as their families. In their quest for survival, some of these college graduates immigrate to more developed countries in Europe and the United States where they can afford a better quality of life.

Acculturation and Culturally Responsive Teaching

In order to live the good life they seek and desire, immigrants soon realize that life in diaspora is not a bed of roses. In America, they often have to assimilate by acquiring social tools, education, and cultural knowledge. Thus, these college graduates typically head back to a US college or university so they can be fully acculturated in society. *Acculturation* is the process of modifying an individual, group, or people by adapting to another culture. It can also be a merging of cultures over a prolonged period of time through the process of assimilation and immersion into the new culture.

The process of acculturation, be it self or systemic, is subtle, but actively implemented in all spheres, especially in the education of immigrants. However, what is not currently used as much in institutions of higher learning is culturally relevant teaching (CRT). Culturally responsive teaching (Gay 2010; 2013), or culturally responsive pedagogy (CRP) (Ladson-Billings 1995), is an approach to teaching that recognizes the importance of students' cultural references in learning spaces.

Brown (2003) describes it as a teaching that is conscious of the soci-ocultural diversities of learners. Ladson-Billings (2005) suggests that CRP is lacking in higher education because few models are available to inform the practice in higher education. Others believe that the lack is due to overreliance on institutional cultures within higher education that is derived from societal structures (Gay 2010).

METHOD

Participants were purposefully selected from a Nigerian community in a southeastern state of the United States. Of the thirty people contacted, only eight indicated interest, but three later dropped out of the study for personal reasons. Participants' selection was based on five criteria: each participant a) is a Nigerian college graduate, b) has completed at least their undergraduate degree in Nigeria, c) has graduated with additional degree(s) from United States' higher education institutions, d) is between twenty-five and forty-five years of age, and e) is a resident in this particu-lar southeastern state at the time of the study. The five participants in-cluded three males and two females.

A narrative case study design was used to capture the different dimen-sions of participants' lived experiences. This process of inquiry was used to systematically gather and analyze the data collected from participants' through a) their responses to semi-structured interview questions and b) through open conversations with the researcher during which participants shared their lived experiences.

Additional data from participants' dialogue and description were col-lected as field notes. The goal of using this method of inquiry was to capture the different dimensions of participants' lived experiences: from their accounts of the various social relationships, their individual environ-mental and cultural contexts (Clandinin and Connelly 2000). The inter-views lasted between forty-five and ninety minutes at locations of partici-pants' choice.

FINDINGS

Three main themes emerged from the participants' stories: 1) family expectations, 2) survival mechanism, and 3) cultural relevancy in American higher education. Each participant's story showcased family expectations and the motivation to earn a college degree. Their experiences indicated that earning a college degree in their homeland did not always translate into gainful employment, but it was culturally expected and sometimes dictated by the society. The same societal demands were subtly experienced in the context in which they found themselves in the United States of America.

Family Expectations

Families in Nigeria often place high expectations on their children. These expectations sometimes mean that family members can direct their children toward career disciplines such as medicine, engineering, law, pharmacy, etc. The huge expectation placed on the graduate often results in a lot of pressure due to the low income per family and non-availability of jobs.

Participants' Stories

Alice graduated with a bachelor of medicine and bachelor of surgery (MBBS) degree in pediatrics before immigrating to the United States. The MBBS is equivalent to doctor of medicine (MD). After working odd jobs for a couple of years, she decided to enroll in a US university where she earned a medical degree in child and adolescent psychiatry. After completing her residency, she proceeded to obtain her fellowship in the same field. Alice went back to school because the degree she had from Nigeria was not accepted for medical practice in the United States. She stated:

> Growing up in Nigeria, my desire was to study Theater Arts, but it was not well received by my family; my family did not appreciate that. They wanted me to be a lawyer, a doctor, or an engineer. Particularly my uncle, who was my school principal, and my high school teacher, both wanted me to be a doctor. They pressured me to be a doctor, with

promises, some they fulfilled, some they didn't (*laughs*). That's how I got into the medical field. Although my family encouraged me toward studying medicine, the financial demands created a lot of economic hardship for us.

Similarly, **James**, who currently works as a personal computer engineer in a communication company, completed a degree in electrical engineering prior to immigrating to the United States. Upon arrival in the United States, he enrolled in a university where he graduated with an electrical engineering degree. He shared:

> I studied engineering because that was what my family wanted for me. It meant I would make more money when I get a job. My family expected me to graduate from college and get a job so I can help in taking care of my siblings, my parents, and other family members who contributed to my education.

Emmanuel's story is not different. He is a practicing attorney who earned a bachelor's degree in economics from a Nigerian university. After he arrived in America, he worked multiple entry-level jobs while enrolled in evening classes at a community college. He went back to a liberal arts university from where he graduated with a law degree. He partnered with a law firm for some years before establishing his own. His comments echoed the others:

> Back home children are the social security benefit for their families: you are their safety net, you are their 401k, and you are everything. Great expectations are placed on you upon graduating from college.

Survival Mechanisms

As more graduates are produced in Nigeria and fewer jobs are available to engage their expertise, the youths become restless. The need to pursue a better life and more favorable opportunities became more attractive as an option to escape the challenges. The participants reported disappointments with their inability, or "failures," to meet the expectations of their families, which prompted them to embark on a survival quest in a foreign land.

Jude earned a bachelor of science degree in economics and a master's degree in management in Nigeria before migrating to the United States. With two degrees, his continued unemployment status caused him to seek succor overseas. He moved around different states before he finally secured admission to study accounting. Jude recounts:

> With two degrees, I could not find a job. I struggled with odd jobs, tried starting a business, but nothing worked. I decided to leave for the United States. Don't get me wrong, I struggled here, too, but it was more bearable. I headed back to school, but then I had to change my career path. You know, without an American degree, you know, you ain't getting a good job. It was hard keeping up financially. . . . I had two jobs and was a full-time student. I had to balance work and school. . . . I did not have a life for so long.

Angela's story was not different. She, like the other participants, graduated with a biology and lab technology degree. Her determination to live the American dream led her to enroll in a university after years of working in a retail store. She earned an "American degree" in chemistry, so she can earn a decent living. Her story:

> Challenges in Nigeria were the norm. The demand was huge, especially when you finish your education and you cannot find a job, let alone a well-paying job. You have your family and siblings looking up to you. It is worse if you are the first child in the family. So, the only option was to look for a way out, so you can help out. Life was hard. I was looking for greener pastures; to do something different. I left.

Emmanuel stated:

> When things were not forthcoming for me, I had to leave in order to care for my family. The frustration and uncertainties in Nigeria led to my decision to leave the country.

The road to success did not come easy for these participants. They had to be enculturated, a process of integration and adaptation, into the new society. Arthur (2000) observed that immigrants often find that their degrees are devalued or sometimes cannot be transferred at all, especially in fields such as health care and education. Another survival mechanism had to be utilized.

For the participants, education was their one means of realizing their dreams. **James** reported, "there was uncertainty here too [in the United States] at the beginning, but there are also opportunities. Going back to school was the only way to make it here," and **Alice** noted, "everybody knows that when you come to America, you have to start from the beginning, almost like all over again."

Acculturation and Culturally Responsive Teaching in America's Higher Education

Participants shared stories of their academic challenges in America's higher education. The lack of cultural sensitivity and responsiveness to racial and ethnic diversity in higher institutions of learning created some challenges for the participants. As a trained medical doctor before emigrating to the United States, **Alice** recalled:

> Despite the fact that I was a practicing medical doctor before I came here [America], as a "new medical student" or maybe during my residency, there was this occasion when they wanted to draw blood from a patient, but there was no phlebotomist around. I volunteered to draw the blood but was denied because I was "not qualified" to do the procedure. What I knew or my cultural background was never included (*laughs*) . . . was never a part of my teaching because you know . . . it was considered inferior or inadequate.

Likewise **Jude** pointed out:

> Going back to school after I got here [United States] was challenging. You were expected to know stuff the American way. No one cared about what you know or came to class with. Because I was new to the system, some examples used in the lectures were foreign to me . . . when you ask for help, they look down at you, like you don't know anything. It was sometimes frustrating . . . but with your goal in mind, you have to pass the class, you just have to push through and work harder.

Participants also reported being penalized for using British spellings, which was part of their educational training, so they had to learn fast to use American spellings. Andrade (2006) determines that "even though negative incidents provoked feelings of embarrassment, frustration, disappointment and boredom, international students responded with constructive behaviors including a variety of study strategies" (135). **Angela** stated:

> Going back to school in America was not easy for me, however, what I found most challenging or sometimes difficult to handle, was how you are looked at as ignorant if you say or write things that don't sound American. I learned with British English and writing, so my spellings were sometimes not the same . . . you know to them [instructors], our culture or education does not count.

DISCUSSION

The purpose of this study was to gain understanding of how culture, scholarship, and survival intersect to influence and shape the lives of participants in this study. The findings suggest that all the participants had common struggles and challenges that are rooted in these three components. Their narratives suggest that: 1) the burden placed on them by their families and society propelled them to seek ways of survival; 2) survival for them meant leaving their homeland in search of greener pastures in the West; and 3) survival in a foreign land meant re-educating themselves so they could have meaningful lives in their country of abode.

Their stories portray how extenuating factors helped in shaping them through their journey. Their home culture laden with family expectation and societal pressure, propelled their exodus to pursue better lives for themselves and their families, and confronted the cultural challenges in America's higher education. They learned to navigate through the cultural obstacles, achieving their scholastic goals using survival tools to reach their anticipated destinies.

CONCLUSION

The immigrants in this study shared stories of their lived experiences as college graduates in Nigeria and in the United States of America. Their survival stories may not be different or isolated from those experienced by other immigrants from developing countries who seek better lives, but their stories are sometimes misrepresented and often times mislabeled.

This study sheds light on some inadequate representation of facts concerning immigrants from non-White countries.

Despite the struggles and challenges faced by these immigrants, they often showed resilience and the will to survive. They forge ahead, most returning to school to earn degrees they already have, to earn an "American degree" that will give them better opportunities for gainful employment. Coulombe and Tremblay (2009) note that workers trained at destination countries enjoy higher wages and employment rates than their counterparts from other countries.

These stories portray an intersection of culture, scholarship, and survival. As the debate on immigration continues, it is important to provide information that is factual to prevent misrepresentations that can be perpetuated in our national discourse. Rong and Brown (2002) note that the "lack of research on Black immigrants denies the American public and policy makers opportunities to explore the many urgent and intriguing issues concerning Black immigrants" (249). The rhetoric then continues to focus on misinformation and false assumptions. Culturally relevant teaching that respects and embraces the cultural and ethnic diversity in our institutions of learning is one way to foster change.

REFLECTIVE QUESTIONS
FOR CULTURALLY RESPONSIVE TEACHERS WORKING
WITH IMMIGRANT STUDENTS

1. As educators, what challenges do you face in teaching non-White immigrant students and how do you navigate through these challenges?
2. What major challenge(s) are faced by non-white immigrant students in America's institutions of learning?
3. How can institutions of learning mitigate these challenges to ensure equitable learning opportunities for these students?
4. How can culturally responsive/relevant teaching be used to accommodate the cultural, racial, ethnic, etc., differences of today's learners?

5. What support systems, accommodations, or awareness are available for non-White immigrant students in higher institutions of learning?
6. How can educators change the narratives that inaccurately portray non-White immigrants?

REFERENCES

Adepoju, A. 2008. *Migration and Social Policy in Sub-Saharan Africa*. United Nations Research Institute for Social Development (UNRISD). Working paper.

Andrade, M. S. 2006. "International Students in English-Speaking Universities: Adjustment Factors." *Journal of Research in International Education* 5 (2): 131–54.

Arthur J. A. 2000. *Invisible Sojourners: African Immigrant Diaspora in the United States*. Westport, CT: Praeger.

Brown, D. F. 2003. "Urban Teachers' Use of Culturally Responsive Management Strategies." *Theory into Practice* 42 (4): 277–82.

Clandinin, D. J., and F. M. Connelly. 2000. *Narrative Inquiry: Experience and Story in Qualitative Research*. San Francisco: Jossey-Bass.

Coulombe, S., and J. F. Tremblay. 2009. "Migration and Skills Disparities across the Canadian Provinces." *Regional Studies* 43 (1): 5–18.

Development Research Centre (DRC), Global Migrant Origin Database. 2007. "Migration." Retrieved from http://www.migrationdrc.org/research/typesofmigration/globalmigrantorigindatabase.html.

Dumont, J., and G. Lemaître. 2005. *Counting Immigrants and Expatriates in OECD Countries: A New Perspective*. Organisation for Economic Co-Operation and Development. OECD Social, Employment and Migration working papers.

Fu, L. 2017. "Nearly Half of Immigrants Enter the US with a College Degree." Fortune.com, July 5. Retrieved from http://fortune.com/2017/07/05/us-immigrants-education/.

Gay, G. 2010. *Culturally Responsive Teaching: Theory, Research, and Practice*. 2nd ed. New York: Teachers College Press.

Gay, G. 2013. "Teaching To and Through Cultural Diversity." *Curriculum Inquiry* 43 (1): 48–70.

Ijaiya, B. 2007. "Addressing Youth Unemployment through Entrepreneurship Education." *Ilorin Journal of Education* 27: 54—60.

International Labour Organization. 2007. *Global Employment Trends Brief*. Geneva: ILO.

Ladson-Billings, G. 1995. "Toward a Theory of Culturally Relevant Pedagogy." *American Educational Research Journal* 32 (3): 465–91.

Ladson-Billings, G. 2005. "The Evolving Role of Critical Race Theory in Educational Scholarship." *Race Ethnicity and Education* 8 (1): 115–19.

Migration Policy Institute. 2014. *National Center for Immigration Integration Policy*. Retrieved from https://cis.org/Migration-Policy-Institute-MPI.

National Academies of Sciences, Engineering, and Medicine. 2015. *The Integration of Immigrants into American Society*. Washington, DC: The National Academies.

Nesbitt, N. F. 2002. "African Intellectuals in the Belly of the Beast: Migration, Identity, and the Politics of Exile." *African Issues* 30 (1): 70–75.

New American Economy. 2018. *International Students*. Retrieved from http://www.newamericaneconomy.org/.

Ngoma, A. L., and N. W. Ismail. 2013. "The Determinants of Brain Drain in Developing Countries." *International Journal of Social Economics* 40 (8): 744–54.

Okon, U., A. Udofia, T. Udofia, and A. G. Udofia. 2007. *Curricular Provisions for Universities and Professional Skills Development in Nigeria.* Education Research Network for West and Central African (ERNWACA), 1–45.

Porter, M. E. 1990. *The Comparative Advantage of Nations.* New York: The Free Press.

Portes, A., and R. Rumbaut. 2006. "Front Matter." In *Immigrant America: A Portrait,* i–iv. 3rd edition. Revised, expanded, and updated. Berkeley: University of California Press. Retrieved from http://www.jstor.org/stable/10.1525/j.ctt1pq07x.1.

Rong, X. L., and F. Brown. 2002. "Socialization, Culture, and Identities of Black Immigrant Children." *Education and Urban Society* 34 (2): 247–73.

United Nations Development Program (UNDP). 2010. "Nigerian Migration Report." Retrieved from https://esa.un.org/miggmgprofiles/indicators/files/Nigeria.pdf.

U.S. Census Bureau. 2008–2012. "American Community Survey Briefs: Characteristics of Selected Sub-Saharan African and Caribbean Ancestry Groups." Retrieved from https:www.census.gov/programs-surveys/acs/.

The World Bank. 2007. *Global Economic Prospects 2007: Managing the Next Wave of Globalization.* Global Economic Prospects. Washington, DC: The World Bank. Retrieved from https://openknowledge.worldbank.org/handle/10986/7157.

The World Bank. 2011. *Migration and Remittances Factbook.* Washington, DC: The World Bank.

Yaqub, H. 2007. "The Brain Drain Phenomenon in Nigeria and the Struggles by the Academic Staff Union of Universities (ASUU) to Redress It." A seventeen-page paper presented at a conference of University Chancellors in Abuja, Nigeria.

3

CULTURALLY RESPONSIVE LEADERSHIP DEVELOPMENT PROJECT FOR MENTAL HEALTH AND RESILIENCE

A Case Study of Bhutanese-Nepali Women in Central Ohio

Binaya Subedi, Arati Maleku, and Sudarshan Pyakurel

Currently, an estimated 65.6 million people around the world are displaced from their homes. Twenty-two and a half million are refugees (UNHCR 2017). While refugees may or may not share similar experiences as immigrants, it is critical to recognize that refugees are pushed out of their homelands and go through multiple displacements (Kunz 1973). As refugee communities resettle into new geographical locations, they face numerous challenges in adjusting to new environments. Lack of employment and reliable social services, language barriers, and psychosocial stressors are some of the critical issues refugee communities face as they resettle into new spaces (Ellis et al. 2016).

Refugees also experience persistent social isolation and discrimination from the mainstream "host" societies. For example, immigrant and refugee communities who have resettled find the current political climate in the United States to be hostile toward their identity and ways of knowing (Maira 2009). Although literature is evolving in examining post-migration stressors, significant gaps remain in understanding cumulative risk factors refugee communities encounter as they rebuild their lives post-migration.

Little is known about protective factors refugee communities utilize when they are resettled in US cities. This complex understanding of cumulative migration stressors—including historical trauma and mental-health and protective factors—are critical, not only for the development of mental health prevention and intervention programs, but also to develop human service capacity and infrastructure that can deliver culturally responsive programs.

Prior studies have emphasized how the use of community strengths and resilience factors can be effective paths to finding solutions to complex challenges that refugee communities face (Papadopoulos 2007). Effective community interventions have been found to reduce psychological distress for Bhutanese refugees better than traditional case management services (Mitschke, Aguirre, and Sharma 2013; Reiffers et al. 2013). Gerber and colleagues (2017) found that Bhutanese refugees that participated in community gardening programs experienced feeling well adjusted to living in the United States and were more aware of refugee status requirements (e.g., obtaining necessary documentations, adhering to medical examination requirements).

Bhutanese refugee women who had engaged in financial literacy and knitting groups also showed decreased symptoms of post-traumatic stress disorder (PTSD), anxiety, depression, and somatization (Mitschke et al. 2013). There are limited research studies that address how Bhutanese or Bhutanese-Nepali youth, particularly girls and women, come to experience life in the United States, including the challenges they face in social and educational spheres. Maira (2009) determines that immigrant youth face challenges in negotiating educational curriculum/culture and often find it difficult to negotiate supportive and safe spaces in US society.

This chapter highlights research and community work with Bhutanese-Nepali youth, particularly women, in relation to developing a culturally responsive leadership program. The leadership project was organized for two semesters. Each cohort had approximately thirty students who attended high school or local colleges. Students were invited to participate through community nominations. The program explored the value of developing a leadership program that was based on culturally responsive curriculum and documented the importance of developing a leadership program that reflected community needs and experiences. This chapter further reflects on how a culturally responsive program was used to promote leadership skills, knowledge about US social structures and community advocacy.

In addition to migration challenges faced by families, the project sought to document how Bhutanese-Nepali women in the United States faced myriad challenges such as identity struggles, social isolation, discrimination, and difficulties in adapting to new conditions and structures. The youth faced barriers to developing a sense of cultural identity and exerting their sense of agency because of community mental health concerns. Based on community needs, given the stress of resettlement and the challenges faced by youth, a culturally responsive leadership project was implemented to empower young Bhutanese women as cultural leaders.

The teaching approach focused on engaging with social justice issues and valuing community knowledge and experiences. The project similarly sought to empower the youth so that they could question status quo in US society and also engage with the challenges faced by the community. In particular, the program was developed so that youth could utilize community assets and cultural resources, which can serve as protective factors to challenge gender norms, promote mental well-being, and build community resilience.

THE CULTURALLY RESPONSIVE LEADERSHIP (CRL) PROJECT

The intervention research project utilized knowledge within the community to co-learn and co-develop culturally responsive curriculum for the leadership development of high school and college-aged women within the Bhutanese-Nepali community. The researchers examined three important components that formed the basis of the cultural leadership project: (1) recognition of the history of the community, particularly around issue of displacement, collective struggles, and experiences; (2) incorporation of mental health challenges as a critical component to building community resilience and leadership; (3) development of culturally responsive themes on leadership development that incorporated community needs, assets, and concerns.

The overarching goal of the project was to enhance cultural leadership skills so that women could be active subjects within and outside of their communities. Community participation was at the heart of the project. In collaboration with the Bhutanese Nepali Community Organization, the project was co-developed based on the community's concerns over: a) the lack of formal education that women had received historically; b) the limited leadership positions that were held by Bhutanese women within and outside of community; c) the challenges Bhutanese women faced in US society in cultural, health, political, and economic domains.

THE BHUTANESE COMMUNITY
AND COMMUNITY HISTORY AND EXPERIENCES

Educators who work with refugee youth and their families need to critically understand the history of how a community has come to resettle in a particular space, particularly around how oppression shapes forced migration experiences. This historical understanding can provide critical insights into how youth have come to understand the role of schools or how parents or guardians approach educational and social spaces. The learning and the unlearning of history enables a better understanding about cultural practices and how historical events shape people's ways of being and knowing.

The starting point of the project was engaging with how displacement had shaped the community's experience. In the context of Bhutanese community, the category of displacement includes how communities have been unrooted from their ancestral homes and have faced various forms of discrimination. It speaks about how displacement has taken place, why it took place, and how the migration to a new nation-state creates challenges for the community. It also speaks about the ways in which the community has survived the violence of displacement and the trauma regarding the loss of rights/identity and ancestral homeland.

The United States resettled a 79,000 Bhutanese-Nepali population from 2008 to 2014 (Ellis et al. 2016). The region of Central Ohio, where the leadership project was developed, is home to approximately 23,427 Bhutanese-Nepali community members (Adhikari et al. 2015). Due to secondary and tertiary migrations from other states, the population is predicted to increase over the next five years with the community potentially comprising 30,000 to 40,000 members (S. Pyakurel, personal communication, January 20, 2017).

Clearly, the successful adaptation of refugees to a particular space is conditional upon individual and societal circumstances, including factors related to pre-migration, migration, and resettlement experiences. While factors such as family structure, mental health, prior exposure to trauma, level of education, gender, age, and employment play a role in adaptation, societal factors including, but not limited to, social support, family support, and host community responses (for example, discrimination) impact adaptation experiences (Ellis et al. 2016). The adaptation experience for refugee communities is strongly correlated to their overall mental well-being and the ways in which they are able to negotiate social structures in the arrival city.

By learning about historical context of forced migration, educators can come to recognize the complexity of identity that displaced communities have to navigate and the ways of being/knowing that members of the community embrace. The Nepali-speaking Bhutanese community lived in the southern part of Bhutan for more than five generations and was treated as a perpetual outsider in their country of birth. In Bhutan, the community was identified or referred as Lhotshampas (people of South); however, in the US context, Bhutanese and Bhutanese-Nepali are interchangeably used to identify the group because of the community's dual identity: embodying both Nepali and Bhutanese cultural and linguistic identities.

The researchers used the Bhutanese-Nepali term to document the voices of youth who negotiate Bhutanese as well as Nepali aspects of identity since most youth we worked with were born and socialized into Nepali aspects of culture and history within schools in Nepal. This interchanging and intertwined identity of the group is also a function of the community's complex cultural identity that emerged out of their complicated history of migration and displacement. Because of the ethnic cleansing policy of the Bhutanese government, the community fled and lived in refugee camps in eastern parts of Nepal. Similarly, even in Nepal, although the community is of Nepali ethnic descent, they were treated as "outsiders." The community was rarely considered part of the mainstream Nepali community, even though it shared a common ancestral identity, language, culture, and traditions with communities in Nepal.

The leadership program emphasized the need to value one's gender, cultural, and linguistic identity. It was based on the idea that when one values (and questions) one's identity, one can begin to critically reflect on one's location or positionality within the social world. Many students identified as being of Nepali descent since they were born in Nepal and were socialized into Nepali culture. The youth indicated that their parents or grandparents identified as being of Bhutanese descent yet sought the preservation of aspects of Nepali language and culture that was connected to Bhutanese ways of being. The youth shared how the very idea that Bhutanese-Nepali families would be re-settled to a third country (the United States, Canada, New Zealand, Denmark, etc.) had never been a possibility growing up in refugee camps.

The third-country settlement united as well as separated families, since many families continued to live in Nepal or desired to return to Bhutan. The leadership program was committed to honoring (and bridging) the complexity of identity and experiences across generations that the youth and the family negotiated because of the community's historical and contemporary experiences. Similar to other refugee experiences, discussion of Bhutanese displacement can't omit questions around structural violence and how the community displacement is an effect of ethnic cleansing policies. The violence a community has endured impacts its mental health, well-being, and how it understands and engages with institutions such as public schools or other state entities.

The Bhutanese government initiated a policy called "One Nation, One People" which aimed to "unite" its citizens via a single national, cultural, and religious identity known as "Bhutanization." Yet this interpretation of national unity sought selective ways of codifying national history and culture, and thus marginalized the ethnic Nepali population's desire to be culturally distinct (including the strong desire to maintain the age-old linguistic and cultural practices). Despite the contribution of the Nepali-speaking community in the building of the country, the policy sought to erase Nepali culture that had survived and prospered for hundreds of years.

Bhutanization undermined the distinct cultural heritage of the people of the South and sought to enforce the ethnic cleansing policy in schools, hospitals, within local and national public offices, and virtually all public and private domains. It required that all people living within the boundaries of Bhutan follow a national code of conduct called "*Diclamnamza.*" The code required that every person be required to wear particular dress that fit under the national policy, speak a particular language (Dzongkha), follow dominant national culture, and forego the age-old Nepali traditions and culture. The "One Nation, One People" policy was not a product of national consensus but of the decisions made by the ruling class of Bhutan.

Educators need to recognize that activism has also been a critical component of the community's experience. In response to the ethnic cleansing policies, various demonstrations and rallies were held in the southern districts of Bhutan in the late 1980s. Similarly, appeals to the King of Bhutan (Jigme Singye Wangchuck) were made to seek justice, equality, and the protection of religion, language, and the traditions of the people in the South. However, viewing the appeals as a threat, the government enforced strict policies in public schools and government offices so that Nepali language and culture was not to be spoken or practiced.

In the early 1990s, government buildings were converted into makeshift army barracks. Subsequently, the Royal Bhutan Army occupied public spaces, began making random arrests, apprehended leaders of the community, and charged them with terrorism. The Nepali speaking community spoke out against the human rights violations and ethnic cleansing policies of the government. Anyone who had participated in rallies, helped in organizing protests, and those who had not followed *Diclamnamza* in general, were imprisoned without due process. Finding no other options, thousands of the Nepali-speaking population fled the country, and by the late 1990s, 100,000 people had left Bhutan for refugee camps in Nepal.

It is worth recognizing that refugee experiences are radically different from other immigrant experiences because of the cultural loss refugee subjects have faced, including trauma related to death of family members, loss of personal property, and loss of one's identification with land (Espiritu 2006). In the Bhutanese-Nepali context, a critical component of students' identities was shaped by their lived experiences within refugee camps. Students noted that twenty-two years was the span of time that families spent in refugee camps and learned to negotiate life without any rights to citizenship. What is common within the Bhutanese refugee experience is the sense of shared identity: identity that is forged based on a cultural and linguistic identity.

The leadership sessions revealed that it is precisely the experience of being displaced, the family and community's experience of pain and survival, that brings the youth together as Bhutanese-Nepali subjects. The strong sense of community spirit was forged over time not only in relation to the physical and emotional pain that individuals have suffered, but also because of the suffering that has taken place in communal ways. There is also a sense of deep ambivalence regarding what may take place in the future, including the uncertainty of what may happen to the larger Bhutanese community that is locally and globally displaced.

MENTAL HEALTH AND WELL-BEING OF THE BHUTANESE-NEPALI POPULATION

Efforts to develop culturally relevant approach to leadership curriculum cannot be separated from mental health concerns, including questions around trauma. Thus, it is critical for educational professionals to meaningfully understand how displacement and trauma impact youth's schooling experiences and their families' ability to understand and respond to school issues. As victims of painful atrocities such as persecution, violence, rape, and torture, refugees are extremely susceptible to psychiatric morbidity and traumatic life events (Fazel, Wheeler, and Danesh 2005).

Post-traumatic stress disorder (PTSD) and depression are widespread within refugee communities, and more likely to occur in refugee populations in comparison to the general population. The Bhutanese population is categorized as an at-risk population due to the continued mental health challenges they face. In addition to anxiety, depression, and PTSD, the community also has one of the highest suicide rates, not only among refugee groups, but also within the general US population.

Once resettled, the Bhutanese community has faced a myriad of hardships and psychosocial stressors such as concerns about employment, reliable social services, and language barriers (Ellis et al. 2016). Discussion with the youth highlighted how the current anti-immigrant political climate in the United States has further created stress on Bhutanese families. Many youth shared that mainstream people they met in daily life harbored deep animosity toward refugee and immigrant subjects.

During the leadership sessions, mental health was a recurring topic of discussion, particularly how women faced multiple challenges in migration contexts. Recent studies conducted by the Centers for Disease Control and Prevention (Cochran et al. 2013) and the Ohio Mental Health and Addiction Services (Adhikari et al. 2015) suggest alarming rates of anxiety symptoms, PTSD, depression, suicide, and substance use among Bhutanese population. The study in Ohio (Adhikari et al. 2015) found high levels of exposure to trauma and a low rate of self-identified mental health conditions, revealing unmet mental health treatment needs that are either not spoken or under-reported by participants.

The challenges faced by the community highlight the critical need in behavioral health interventions through culturally and linguistically appropriate services, including educational outreach approaches that can benefit the community. Similar to historically marginalized communities in the United States, the community has also shown less desire to seek mental health services. For example, in their study, Adhikari et al. (2015) noted how less than a third (28 percent) of the study group was interested in seeking help from a mental health professional or medical practitioner.

The women shared that they felt vulnerable to being discriminated against, noted being devalued for what they knew, and felt less prepared to navigate US institutions, particularly in their efforts to help their families. Many youth noted that language and cultural barriers as well as discriminations they faced led to their having a sense of low self-esteem. There was agreement in small group conversations that the difficulties of negotiating institutions (schools, employment, etc.) made their families or community members more apprehensive of how the community would negotiate or experience life in the future.

Working with the community, researchers recognized that the issue of mental well-being was one of the most talked about topics, especially with victims of multiple oppressions. Unfortunately, mainstream society often neglects the mental health concerns and trauma faced by marginalized communities. In addition to facing a myriad of hardships in adjusting to their new surroundings, researchers learned that the lack of employment, unreliable social, health, and educational institutions impacted the mental well-being of the community.

Educators point out how the challenges youth face in both in- and out-of-school contexts impact their academic work and the overall schooling experiences (Kumashiro 2004). Among the Bhutanese population, questions about belonging and identity struggles, experience with persistent social isolation, and discriminations in workplaces have been common. The leadership team documented how the difficulties in adapting to new conditions in regards to housing, transportation, health systems, family conflicts, and financial hardships created stress for the families. The arrival and settlement has affected family relationships, particularly the role of girls/women and the nature of challenges they are encountering as well as the possibilities they are creating within their communities. Within this context of mental health concerns amongst the community, the leadership program was grounded on developing culturally relevant leadership curriculum which invited women to be active members within and outside of their communities. It also sought ways to mobilize collective advocacy for community mental health concerns.

CULTURALLY RELEVANT LEADERSHIP CURRICULUM FOR POSITIVE MENTAL WELL-BEING AND RESILIENCE

Considering the historical context of oppression the community has endured and the trauma the community continues to face, the approach centered on developing curriculum that would meet the needs of the youth. The team sought to engage women regarding issues that mattered to them, issues that would be relevant to their lives and their community. This included themes such as women's access to health care, domestic violence, barriers to living wages, and language barriers women faced in everyday contexts.

Developing a transformative curriculum and developing spaces that would enable the youth to not only better understand social issues but also how the group would be able to apply what they had learned, was critically significant. Thus, the overarching goal of the project was to educate and empower women through a culturally responsive project so that they were able to be cultural leaders within and outside of their communities. In addition to the leadership training, the team examined how the identification and use of assets in the community would serve as protective factors to increase resilience and positive mental well-being within the community.

The one-year project developed and delivered two cycles of an educational training program designed to develop leadership skills that could begin to address mental health concerns as well as resilience among Bhutanese-Nepali women. Each cycle (a four- to six-month period) included approximately twenty-five participants, and the curriculum was developed by assessing the specific challenges the community faced so that the project met the needs of individuals and the community. Prior to developing the leadership program, the team assessed the kinds of experiences and challenges participants and the community had encountered, and documented the concerns faced by individual participants. This process allowed for a critical examination and assessment of the leadership needs the women desired and articulated as being significant.

One of the needs documented by the study concerned the lack of critical education youth had received in high school or in college, in examining US social and economic structures. For many women, despite having lived in the United States for more than five to seven years, ways to develop leadership or a critical understanding of US society remained a continual challenge. This was largely due to lack of access to educational and cultural resources or opportunities. Language barriers and lack of mentors in schools and universities often prevented women from accessing resources and becoming critical participants in US society.

Due to the significant gaps in programs that were available for women that addressed leadership skills, the project was designed: (1) to actively engage Bhutanese-Nepali women in their learning processes; (2) to explore women's lived experience to address their mental well-being; and (3) to provide culturally responsive instruction to validate youth's ways of knowing and being. Since, historically, Bhutanese women have not had the opportunity to access economic, health, educational, political, and legal resources, this project was designed to assist in developing and enhancing knowledge/skills within and outside of community contexts.

Developing curriculum and culturally responsive pedagogy was grounded on the historical reality of oppressions faced by the Bhutanese community and the displacement/trauma the community had faced over time. The community had experienced loss of land and citizenship, and the community lived in refugee camps for more than twenty years. Like other historically marginalized communities in the United States, Bhutanese-Nepali youth were facing challenges in accessing educational spaces and claiming citizenship rights in US society.

The project focused on providing leadership development skills as a core component of building resilience which could enable spaces for better (cultural) lived experiences for the Bhutanese community. Consequently, the team focused on several elements within the curriculum that would make it culturally relevant or culturally responsive (Gay 2010). Prior to developing the curriculum for the two-semester-long project, the team engaged in dialogue with many adult members as well as the youth of the community. Based on initial findings, the team focused on the following five areas of curricular emphasis that community members viewed as being critically important: (1) economic/financial literacy; (2) political literacy; (3) legal literacy; (4) health literacy; and (5) school literacy.

Based on the initial conversation, the team recognized how the challenges of understanding legal, political, economic, educational, and health systems became stress factors for the youth as they experienced US society. Their lack of knowledge about social systems in the United States affected the women's mental well-being and placed them on the margins of society, leading to further isolation. The team also critically analyzed how mental well-being affected individual's ability to find employment, stay employed, and desire to perform well in schools/colleges. Therefore, the team was committed to developing a culturally relevant approach to teaching and learning (Ladson-Billings 2010) that would support students' ways of being and knowing, and which valued bilingual and community-based knowledge.

First, the focus on economic literacy was placed in the context of community needs, considering that many families had limited knowledge on how the economic systems worked in the US context. Students often spoke about the challenges their parents faced in finding employment and how Bhutanese women were part of the low wage employment industry. Based on students' sharing of experiences, the team discussed cases that spoke of how (because of the lack of English-language skills) elderly in the community faced numerous financial challenges.

To engage in community dialogue, community members were invited to share how they had successfully navigated employment landscape as well as how they had learned to address financial constraints. Topics included how community members faced challenges in negotiating: credit/debit system, mortgage and lending practices, loans and lease agreements. Many youth felt that, since women managed household systems, financial problems placed more burden on women. A recurring topic of discussion centered on issues of fraud and how elderly members, especially those who had limited English skills, were vulnerable to financial scams.

The topic of community members being exploited became a critical topic of discussion in a number of sessions since this was a topic that students had experienced within their families, or they knew someone who had been exploited. The discussion on community members receiving calls from those claiming to be IRS agents and police created spaces to discuss how many community members had become victims of financial fraud. The topic on the impact of high interest rates (cars, homes, and other purchases) also engendered discussions of everyday financial practices that youth noted their families knew little about.

In the context of political literacy segment, the work engaged culturally relevant approaches to learning about and responding to civic issues. This included discussion of community related cases and how they connected with local political processes; such as ways of contacting local congressional representatives and the mayor's office regarding concerns and needs. Students noted how women needed to work with advocacy groups concerning needs such as affordable housing, safety concerns in neighborhoods, and discrimination faced in schools and workplaces.

A culturally significant case emphasized voting and how many elderly Bhutanese women had recently voted in local elections. Students felt that youth needed to initiate efforts in helping community members register to vote to positively impact community concerns during elections. This was a particularly important issue since most members of the community had never voted in local or national elections because of not having citizenship documents in Bhutan or in Nepal.

Further discussions emphasized national events concerning the anti-immigrant climate that affected the community's well-being. Civic engagement and the need to advocate for community needs was a critical part of the discussion. Students noted that it was important to take part in local marches that concerned gender and immigrant rights, and noted the value of working with other marginalized communities in the city.

Culturally responsive ways of engaging with legal issues concerned addressing challenges that individuals, families, and the community faced in their everyday lives. This approach sought not only to enable the youth to understand legal US discourses but also to question unfair laws. The discussion of cases included analyzing legal issues for solutions to be shared with community members. The youth desired to know more about several legal issues, particularly issues that their families or community members had encountered.

One theme that emerged in the discussion was the need to contest landlord practices that did not respect tenants' rights (e.g., neglecting to repair problems in apartments or not providing security at apartments), and how families could take their landlords to court. Similarly, discussion focused on community cases such as how to work with city or neighborhood associations that restricted community events from taking place in homes. Students cited cases where white neighbors called law enforcement when families held community events, including religious ceremonies and celebrations of family members passing away.

Youth pointed out how many cultural and spiritual events were organized by women within households even though restrictions placed undue burden on women. Another theme concerned topics of immigration and ways in which immigrant and refugee families could question current policies and laws that demonized immigrant and refugee experiences, including the anti-immigrant racism that had become common in US society. The cases enabled spaces to discuss concepts such as the first amendment, due process, advocacy, and ways to work with elected members in local, state, and national levels. Overall, there was agreement that more effort was needed to educate women on laws since most women had limited knowledge about the US legal system and faced barriers to overcome the complex use of (English) legal language.

The fourth area discussed concerned the challenges faced by students, families, and the community regarding education. The discussion included ways that the community could gain knowledge about how the K–12 system operated in the United States, and how women could have access to the higher education system. Many students noted how youth were facing challenges in schools because they lacked language skills and did not have educational support at school to understand the US curriculum. The team discussed cases of youth who had become addicted to alcohol or drugs and dropped out of school.

Youth felt that many girls had the obligation to work because of family needs, and they opted to work since they felt they needed to financially support the family. The experiences or cases shared by students became spaces to think through how Bhutanese-Nepali community organizations could play a key role in advocating for youth concerns. This included the need to meet and advocate for more educational resources with the city council and school personnel. Students also noted the value of sending official communications (for example, emails) so that their concerns could be documented.

A worry for many youth was that their parents did not feel connected to their children's school, and schools often did not engage with parents and the community. Students' perspectives confirmed marginalized students' experiences that schools have not historically valued the knowledge students of color bring into schools (Delpit 2006). Too often, a community's cultural knowledge is not viewed as legitimate knowledge to be learned in educational spaces. They expressed a need to advocate for bilingual approaches to education, including integrating Nepali language programs that validated students' linguistic and cultural ways of being.

The final segment of the curriculum addressed health needs of the community, particularly mental health issues that women faced. The discussion focused on providing knowledge on health resources in the community and ways to improve knowledge and skills to access better health care for women. The challenges the community faced included: (1) health behaviors associated with individual, family and/or community levels, including those related to the external environment, and neighborhood cohesion; (2) interplay of cultural care practices and behaviors with the changing health care resources in the United States; (3) culturally grounded risk and protective mechanisms that affect changes in any mental health issues and other common co-occurring mental health disorders (e.g., depression, PTSD, other anxiety disorders, etc.).

Many mothers found it difficult to identify female doctors they felt comfortable with, and the youth felt they needed to help their parents understand the health care system better. Because of the disconnection with US health care system, parents' relied on alternative medicine. The women found the US health care system difficult to understand, and that medical clinics and hospitals often did not have translators to help families with limited English skills.

The team discussed how various families organized spiritual gatherings and large community events to create a sense of belonging in the new place of arrival. This helped women to cope with the challenges of living in the United States. An important part of the health discussion was the need to advocate for Bhutanese-Nepali women's health concerns and the need to educate the community about health risks.

CONCLUSION

There is a critical need for culturally relevant leadership programs to support the leadership development of Bhutanese-Nepali women. Currently, resettlement programs function with drastically reduced budgets and support because of anti-immigrant and anti-refugee federal and state policies. Programs such as citizenship classes to help immigrant and refugee communities learn English and gain basic knowledge about the United States often do not operate within culturally relevant/responsive frameworks. Similarly, workforce training often does not emphasize culturally grounded leadership and social transformation practices.

The researchers' approach to developing a leadership program utilized cultural responsiveness for understanding community experiences and needs. The approach sought to emphasize knowledge that would help women in the community so that they could seek social change. The engagement created opportunities for women to be critical participants within and outside of their own community. They invited students to speak in Nepali as well as in English and were mindful of how the valuing of community language created productive spaces for learning and unlearning.

The leadership development project created a space to engage in conversation regarding the struggles faced by immigrant and refugee communities in the region and enabled researchers to document the stories that are less prominent in local and national media. This program has implications for how other communities may use or expand upon the model being developed. There is potential for communities to work together on issues of immigrant rights, health, and education. Schools and service providers can better understand the needs and experience of immigrant or refugee women through these projects. There is potential to examine the challenges faced by women in Somali, Latinx, African American, and other communities. Examining the particular needs and interests of communities can lead to developing partnership with various social change organizations.

REFLECTIVE QUESTIONS
FOR CULTURALLY RESPONSIVE TEACHERS WORKING
WITH BHUTANESE-NEPALI COMMUNITIES

1. Why is it important for teachers to develop curriculum that mirrors the experiences of youth and their communities?

2. What barriers may refugee families and communities face in seeking access to productive schooling for their youth in the United States?

3. How can teachers advocate on behalf of new immigrant communities that have limited resources and knowledge of the US educational system?

4. What factors shape mental health concerns within refugee communities?

5. What is the relationship between gender and forced migration?

Note: This publication was supported by The Columbus Foundation, United Way of Greater Columbus, and the Ohio State University through the Connect and Collaborate Grant Program. Its contents are solely the responsibility of the authors and do not necessarily represent the official views of the The Columbus Foundation, United Way of Greater Columbus, or the Ohio State University.

REFERENCES

Adhikari, S. B., K. Yotebieng, J. N. Acharya, and J. Kirsch. 2015. *Epidemiology of Mental Health, Suicide and Post-Traumatic Stress Disorder among Bhutanese Refugees in Ohio, 2014*. Columbus, OH: Department of Mental Health and Addiction Services, Community Refugee and Immigration Services.

Cochran, J., P. L. Geltman, H. Ellis, C. Brown, S. Anderton, J. Montour, et al. 2013. "Suicide and Suicidal Ideation among Bhutanese Refugees—United States, 2009–2012." *Morbidity and Mortality Weekly Report* 62 (26): 533–36.

Delpit, L. 2006. *Other People's Children: Cultural Conflicts in the Classroom*. New York: New Press.

Ellis, B. H., E. N. Hulland, A. B. Miller, C. B. Bixby, B. L. Cardozo, and T. S. Betancourt. 2016. *Mental Health Risks and Resilience among Somali and Bhutanese Refugee Parents*. Washington, DC: Migration Policy Institute.

Espiritu, Y. L. 2006. "Toward a Critical Refugee Study: The Vietnamese Refugee Subject in US Scholarship." *Journal of Vietnamese Studies* 1 (1–2): 410–43.

Fazel, M., J. Wheeler, and J. Danesh. 2005. "Prevalence of Serious Mental Disorder in 7,000 Refugees Resettled in Western Countries: A Systematic Review." *The Lancet* 365 (9467): 1309–14. Retrieved from http://dx.doi.org/10.1016/S0140-6736(05)61027-6.

Gay, G. 2010. *Culturally Responsive Teaching: Theory, Research and Practice*. New York: Teachers College.

Gerber, M. M., J. L. Callahan, D. N. Moyer, M. L. Connally, P. M. Holtz, and B. M. Janis. 2017. "Nepali Bhutanese Refugees Reap Support through Community Gardening." *International Perspectives in Psychology: Research, Practice, Consultation* 6 (1): 17–31.

Kumashiro, K. K. 2004. *Against Common Sense: Teaching and Learning toward Social Justice*. New York: Routledge.

Kunz, E. F. 1973. "The Refugee in Flight: Kinetic Models and Forms of Displacement." *International Migration Review* 7 (2): 125–46.

Ladson-Billings, G. 2010. *Dreamkeepers: Successful Teachers of African American Children.* San Francisco, CA: Jossey-Bass.

Maira, S. 2009. *Missing: Youth, Citizenship, and Empire after 9/11.* Durham, NC: Duke University.

Mitschke, D. B., R. T. P. Aguirre, and B. Sharma. 2013. "Common Threads: Improving the Mental Health of Bhutanese Refugee Women through Shared Learning." *Social Work in Mental Health* 11 (3): 249–66.

Papadopoulos, R. K. 2007. "Refugees, Trauma and Adversity-Activated Development." *European Journal of Psychotherapy and Counseling* 9 (3): 301–12.

Reiffers, R., R. P. Dahal, S. Koirala, R. Gerritzen, N. Upadhaya, N. P. Luitel, S. Bhattarai, and M. J. D. Jordans. 2013. "Psychosocial Support for Bhutanese Refugees in Nepal." *Intervention: International Journal of Mental Health and Psychosocial Support in Conflict Affected Areas* 11 (2): 169–79.

United Nations High Commissioner for Refugees [UNHCR]. 2017. *Figures at a Glance.* Retrieved from http://www.unhcr.org/en-us/figures-at-a-glance.html.

4

A PEDAGOGY OF INQUIRY

Preparing Teachers to Work with Immigrant Families

Christian Winterbottom

In the United States, there are currently three mainstream models of teacher preparation programs. These models are commonly described as (a) knowledge for practice (formal knowledge and theory), (b) knowledge in practice (practical knowledge), and (c) knowledge of practice (use the classroom for intentional investigation) (Cochran-Smith and Lytle 1999).

Knowledge for practice implies that having a greater epistemology leads to a better or more effective pedagogy. Thus, preservice teachers (PSTs) having gained an understanding of theorists, methods, and subject matter should be prepared to enter classrooms and be good teachers, without having the in-field praxis support. This construct distinguishes that the difference between novice and experienced teachers is based merely on the amount and depth of content or methods. However, educators posit that novice teachers do not have enough content or methods to teach effectively (Cochran-Smith and Lytle 1999).

The second conception, knowledge in practice, focuses on practical knowledge, indicating that PSTs will learn while they are observing, collaborating, and reflecting on the practices of more experienced teachers. Although in this method of practice the PSTs are in field at a local school, they are not required to teach a class (although they do have limited experience of working with the students). They cooperate with the teacher, observe how the teacher is instructing his/her class, record their observation, and then reflect on how this practice can help them later in their own classrooms.

Knowledge of practice, the third conception, assumes that through inquiry, PSTs make their own epistemology, and through problematic practice research more effective ways of building pedagogy and informing better collaboration between school and community. In this third style of teacher education, PSTs are asked to examine what problems arise in the classroom and through research, discover better ways that they could improve on what is already happening in the classroom.

Most states in the United States license teachers centered on the completion of knowledge tests rather than their performance in the classroom; thus, utilizing the knowledge for practice philosophy. Therefore, it becomes even more critical for teacher education programs to prepare their PSTs to understand and reflect on the connection between their learning in the university classroom regarding pedagogical practices, diversity and inclusion, and their work with families from outside the United States using culturally responsive teaching (CRT) methodologies. In this chapter, the experiences of immigrant families in early education settings are examined, and through a CRT lens, the question of how to effectively prepare teachers to work with immigrant Japanese families is explored; effective pedagogical strategies and practices are also discussed.

CULTURALLY RESPONSIVE TEACHING

There has been a continuous emphasis on multicultural instruction for over four decades and cultural responsive pedagogy for two decades; however, helping teachers become culturally responsive still continues to challenge teacher educators today (Ladson-Billings 2011). CRT has been defined as a way of engaging students' culture, language, and lived experiences in teaching and learning (Lucas, Villegas, and Freedson-Gonzales 2008).

According to Gay (2000), CRT is substantiated in teachers validating the lived experiences of the students, and building a trusting and caring relationship with them. However, Gay also posits that for PSTs to build a trusting and caring experience with students it is essential to understand the history, background, thoughts, and potential fears that the students bring into the classroom. It is well documented (see Ladson-Billings

1994; Lucas et al. 2008) that teachers need to understand students' cultural, language, and lived experiences to better facilitate their learning and high academic achievement.

With respect to this chapter, the term culturally responsive teaching is used to highlight three major aspects of CRT: (1) cultural relevance and pedagogy is connected to students' cultural backgrounds (Gay 2000); (2) communities of learners construct knowledge inclusive of all students (Villegas and Lucas 2002); and (3) culturally responsive teaching reflects a social justice perspective that challenges assumptions and the status quo (Cochran-Smith 2004).

JAPANESE IMMIGRANT FAMILIES IN THE UNITED STATES

To date, there has been little research on Asian immigrant parents' experiences with early schooling in the United States. The Asian population has grown rapidly since the 1990s in the United States, currently estimated to include 12.5 million people, totaling 4.3 percent of the US population. This broad category includes individuals from China, the Philippines, Japan, Korea, Vietnam, Thailand, Laos, India, Pakistan, and Bangladesh, among other countries. These countries represent diverse cultural traditions, religious practices, and languages (Suárez-Orozco and Carhill 2008).

Specifically, there has been little research conducted on the experiences of young Japanese immigrant children and their families in the field of early childhood education in the US and how teacher educators can best prepare teachers to work with this population of immigrants. Although they are highly invested in their children's education, many Japanese parents are satisfied with their roles as helpers at home (Winterbottom 2012). Consequently, many Japanese parents do not regard themselves as equal partners with teachers in their children's education, as culturally this is dissimilar to the roles that occur in their home country. Therefore, once they enter the education system in the United States, many lack the necessary collaboration and informational skills to work effectively with the teachers (Winterbottom 2012).

The role of immigrant parents and teachers collaborating is therefore an intriguing problem for teacher educators to work with. It is difficult for immigrant parents to work with early childhood professionals and educators when neither of these groups have sufficient training to build productive partnerships (Sohn and Wang 2006). How then, do teacher educators help create a community of learners within and outside the university classroom to make all partners successful in their roles?

EARLY CHILDHOOD EDUCATION EXPERIENCES IN JAPAN AND THE UNITED STATES

The number of children attending an early childhood program in Japan is comparatively similar to that of the United States among five-year-olds. In 2016, some 42 percent of three-year-olds, 66 percent of four-year-olds, and 86 percent of five-year-olds were enrolled in pre-primary programs (McFarland et al. 2018). In comparison, preschools in Japan have become an important part of society as 90 percent of all children spend time in one of the two types of preschool: *yochi-en* (nursery) or *hoiku-en* (kindergarten) (Hellman 2016). However, despite the similarities in the number of children enrolled in early childhood education programs across the two countries, the actual classroom/school activities look remarkably different.

In Japan, nature-based activities in early childhood education have been a part of the governmental rules since the early twentieth century, and have been included in the national guidelines since 1926 (Inoue 2014). On average, children in Japan have access to outside activities for just over two hours each day, and many of the programs have garden beds, wild grasses, fruit trees, and plants with flowers and leaves that children can pick and use while playing. Although a playground in the United States may have these natural items in them, the time dedicated to outdoor activities has been remarkably decimated since 2001 (Winterbottom and Lake 2013).

Many early childhood programs in the United States have a strong focus on individualism and creating an "I" identity in the classroom (Winterbottom 2012). However, this has been difficult for families of Japanese children living in the United States, who value a more collectivist approach, where the greater classroom is of importance. Although living in the United States, many Japanese still place high value upon care, responsibility, and being part of a group (Nagase and Kuramochi 2011). In what ways can teachers in the United States work with Japanese immigrant students and their families to meet the educational learning needs of the students?

METHODOLOGY

Participants

This study included eleven participating mothers and fifteen students from Japan who had recently immigrated to the United States. Recent immigrants are defined in this study as those who came to the United States within the past ten years (Douglas-Hall and Koball 2004). Japanese mothers were chosen for several reasons. First, Japanese immigrant mothers differ from their American counterparts on a number of factors.

As mentioned previously, there is strong evidence that Japanese mothers express less confidence in their parenting abilities than do mothers in other industrialized countries. Furthermore, Japanese mothers living in the United States represent a contrast between Eastern and Western cultures, which are different in terms of history, beliefs, and values. It has also been widely documented that immigrants from Asia have replaced Europeans as the majority immigrant group in the United States, but receive little attention in current research (Cote and Bornstein 2009).

DATA COLLECTION AND ANALYSIS

Data collection employed multiple sources including: observations, field notes, semi-structured interview questions, and focus group discussions. The interviews occurred in familiar settings recommended by the mothers, so they could feel comfortable during the research study. Moreover, the interviews lasted approximately one hour in length.

Data obtained from the focus group and in-depth interviews were transcribed verbatim and subsequently analyzed. The interviews were read and reread several times, and memos were written while reading through the transcripts. Specifically, each participant's transcript, phrases, words, thoughts, feelings, or patterns that were common or repeated were circled, highlighted, and color coded (Bogdan and Biklen 2002). Lincoln and Guba (1985) argue that data analysis begins the same day data collection begins in order to facilitate the emergent design, theory, and subsequent data collection.

The semi-structured interview questions provided the initial codes, which were then merged into common themes. A graduate student from the School of Teacher Education also coded the interviews; after coding, both sets of transcripts were compared to ensure dependability and reliability of the data. The observations and field notes were reviewed, coded, and sorted according to the emerging themes and ideas. Codes were sorted into groups that shared the same theme and were created while taking field notes at the site.

DISCUSSION

Two major themes that emerged from the ongoing data analysis, teacher-parent interactions and building relationships, are presented in the following discussion. Under each theme I present various sub-themes that emerged, and offer ways in which each can be addressed in preparing teachers and immigrant parents to work together to form an alliance for positive student learning and growth. They are examples of strategies and resources teachers can use in their work with Japanese immigrant families.

TEACHER-PARENT INTERACTIONS

The teachers are always busy, and we don't really have a lot of time. I just drop him off and pick him up. That's it. Once the preschool told me that I should probably speak with the teacher [Shauna], but she didn't really have a lot of time. She has thirty kids, looking after them, and that is quite a lot.
—Asako

Communication

The statement from Asako was consistent with the other parents' responses regarding their interactions with their children's teachers. Analysis from this study suggested that communication between immigrant parents and teachers (and the PSTs) in the classroom was the key to enhancing a child's participation in an early childhood education (ECE) classroom. Teachers and parents, for example, could plan parent-child activity sessions to be carried out within the school where English would be spoken. These joint activities might prompt more utterances in English, for mothers as well as for the children (Rodriguez-Valls 2016).

Moreover, families and teachers should work together to create meaningful partnerships to support children's development and learning (Mushi 2002). Teachers and parents could create a variety of opportunities for both program teachers and parents to learn more about each other, the children's strengths and needs, and potential parent roles in helping to enhance their learning. Using an approach like this that focuses on the students' cultural backgrounds highlights one of the CRT pedagogies posited by Gay (2000) and Sleeter and Grant (2000). For example, volunteering in the classroom, making decisions about programmatic issues, or advocating for their children's education would help create partnerships that both parents and teachers could benefit from.

Establishing Early Education and Family Literacy Programs

For immigrant children whose first language is not English, preschool programs that prepare children for English language instruction in the elementary school grades could be essential in promoting school readiness (Yaden, Salazar, and Brassell 2003). With this in mind, it has been suggested that family literacy programs should be designed to engage parents by offering English language instruction and workforce skills for adults (Winterbottom 2012).

Improve Teacher Preparation to Work with Immigrant Children

Currently, there is not a lot of in-service or preservice training/professional development that assists teachers in learning how to work with Japanese immigrant children (Winterbottom 2012). In addition, these programs should include a strong curriculum informed by research and the provision of incentives for well-qualified and experienced teachers to teach culturally diverse students. This would improve the education system for young immigrant children.

Encourage Parental Engagement in Schools

Efforts to engage parents in supporting the education of their children are critical, but face many barriers. For example, school cultures can work against large-scale parent engagement because they are usually focused on how parents can help them (the school) rather than vice versa (García-Coll and Szalacha 2004). Also, teacher education programs typically do not prepare teachers to reach out to and engage parents as partners in the education of their children.

The long and non-traditional work schedules of many immigrant parents, and language barriers between parents and educators, can add to the difficulties. García-Coll and Szalacha (2004) believe that teacher preparation programs that provide skills to engage parents in the education of their children from an early age must be a higher priority in the ECE field. Moreover, developing community-based efforts that involve parents in their children's schools and education can help tremendously.

Improve Outreach and Services to All Preschoolers in Immigrant Families

Currently, there are few outreach efforts to immigrant and racial/ethnic minority families. These efforts are usually made by already developed programs such as Head Start/Early Head Start. However, these types of programs are lacking in high-needs communities (Takanishi 2004). If more outreach and services are made to immigrant families, it is likely to result in increased services to immigrant and minority children who have the right to services under the Individuals with Disabilities Education Act.

Recruiting and Retaining Suitable Staff

It has been identified that culturally and linguistically diverse families respond more positively to program staff who reflect their cultural backgrounds or who speak their native languages (Bruns and Corso 2001). Conversely, in the case of the participants in this study, finding Japanese-speaking teachers or teachers who understand Japanese culture, is very difficult. None of the mothers, however, mentioned that they volunteer in the classroom, or have been asked to help with activities. Although barriers may prevent program staff from mirroring the cultures and languages of participating families, Bruns and Corso urge programs to aim for such matching in order to increase trust between programs and families.

BUILDING RELATIONSHIPS

> I moved to this area, so I didn't know about it [a family, childcare, home]. But, my husband is from here so he knows about it from ten years ago. We have family, but most of the family works, so we are looking for long-term care. So, they didn't have any spaces. So, I started looking for by myself. Then, I go to some school, but I am not sure about it.
> —Maya

Locating Resources for Japanese Immigrant Families

Maya's response referred to her family's need to find suitable childcare services for her child. Although a decade ago the United States did not have programs in place that could aid Japanese immigrants who need educational supports (Takanishi 2004), today, the available resources have increased. The literature on providing resources for immigrant families revolves around providing information as well as support for the families.

Communicating through Writing

The mothers identified a lack of communication with the teachers as a barrier in helping their children succeed in preschool. A formal way of bridging this lack of communication is through the written medium. In addition to notes, newsletters, and helpful articles, many immigrant families communicate through email and could be contacted this way.

Creating a Sense of Community

Another strategy for overcoming barriers with immigrant families is creating a sense of belonging (Gonzalez-Mena 2007). This could incorporate such policies as having an *open-door* procedure and/or involving parents in activities that occur at the preschool. In some classrooms, it is common for the teacher to introduce family-tree boards where the children bring in pictures of their family members.

Ongoing Conversations with Families

Although language has been cited as a problem for both parents and teachers, face-to-face interaction is still very important. During the morning at drop-off, or later in the day at pick-up, teachers should make time to speak with parents directly to discuss the welfare of their children. Even if it were something small, the families would be encouraged and would appreciate having the feeling of being a part of the preschool.

Family Participation

Empowering immigrant parents should be one of the key goals in introducing family participation into a preschool program (Gonzalez-Mena 2007). Involving parents in such activities as being a board member, volunteering in the classroom, and participating in other school functions should be something the schools strive toward. However, if the parents are forced to participate this defeats the stated goal of empowerment; so, communication with the families concerning their preferred level of involvement is paramount.

CONCLUSION

This chapter has examined the experiences of immigrant families in early childhood education and provided strategies that teachers could put into place when working with these families. The issues immigrant families face when working in an alien education system can be daunting, and are issues that the author of this chapter has faced twice. Culturally responsive teaching (CRT) is one way of engaging students and parents in education by using their culture, language, and lived experiences.

Through collaborating with the immigrant families, teachers can help their immigrant students succeed in ways they did not think possible. According to Gay (2000), CRT is substantiated by teachers validating the lived experiences of the students, and building a trusting and caring relationship with them. Through their interactions, the teachers can build these relationships, working with the families and their children, to create a positive learning community.

QUESTIONS FOR TEACHERS TO CONSIDER

1. What can I do in my classroom that would be welcoming for immigrant families?
2. How can I communicate effectively with immigrant students and their families?
3. What opportunities can I provide for families to engage them in my classroom?
4. What would a community of learners look like in my classroom? How can I effectively create a learning community that includes all children?
5. How would I work with the administration to ensure I receive the support I need to work with immigrant students and their families?

REFERENCES

Bogdan, R., and S. K. Biklen. 2002. *Qualitative Research for Education: An Introduction to Theories and Methods*. Boston: Allyn and Bacon.

Bornstein, M. H., O. M. Haynes, H. Azuma, C. Galperin, S. Maital, M. Ogino, et al. 1998. "A Cross-National Study of Self-Evaluations and Attributions in Parenting: Argentina, Belgium, France, Israel, Italy, Japan, and the United States." *Developmental Psychology* 34 (4): 662–76.

Bruns, D. A., and R. M. Corso. 2001. *Working with Culturally and Linguistically Diverse Families*. ERIC Digest. Champaign–Urbana, IL: ERIC Clearinghouse on Elementary and Early Childhood Education.

Cochran-Smith, M. 2004. "The Problem of Teacher Education." *Journal of Teacher Education* 55 (4): 295–99.

Cochran-Smith, M., and S. L. Lytle. 1999. "Relationships of Knowledge and Practice: Teacher Learning in Communities." *Review of Research in Education* 24 (1): 249–305.

Cote, L. R., and M. H. Bornstein. 2009. "Child and Mother Play in Three US Cultural Groups: Comparisons and Associations." *Journal of Family Psychology* 23 (3): 355–63.

Douglas-Hall, A., and H. Koball. 2004. "Children of Low-Income, Recent Immigrants." Retrieved from http://www.nccp.org/publications/pub_609.html.

García-Coll, C., and L. A. Szalacha. 2004. "The Multiple Contexts of Middle Childhood." *The Future of Children* 14 (2): 81–97.

Gay, G. 2000. *Culturally Responsive Teaching: Theory, Research and Practice*. New York: Teachers College Press.

Gonzalez-Mena, J. 2007. *Foundations of Early Childhood Education*. New York: McGraw-Hill.

Hellman, A. 2016. "Teaching Reflective Care in Japanese Early Childhood Settings." *Early Child Development and Care* 186 (10): 1693–1702.

Inoue, M. 2014. "Perspectives on Early Childhood Environmental Education in Japan: Rethinking for a Sustainable Society." In *Research in Early Childhood for Sustainability: International Perspectives and Provocations*, edited by J. Davies and S. Elliot, 87–95. London: Routledge.

Ladson-Billings, G. J. 2011. "Is Meeting the Diverse Needs of All Students Possible?" *Kappa Delta Pi Record* 48 (1): 13–15.

Ladson-Billings, G. 1994. *The Dreamkeepers: Successful Teachers of African American Children*. San Francisco: Jossey-Bass.

Lincoln, Y., and E. Guba. 1985. *Naturalistic Inquiry*. Newbury Park, CA: Sage.

Lucas, T., A. M. Villegas, and M. Freedson-Gonzales. 2008. "Linguistically Responsive Teacher Education: Preparing Classroom Teachers to Teach English Language Learners." *Journal of Teacher Education* 59 (4): 361–79.

McFarland, J., B. Hussar, X. Wang, J. Zhang, K. Wang, A. Rathbun, A. Barmer, E. F. Cataldi, and M. F. Bullock. 2018. *The Condition of Education 2018* (NCES 2018-144). U.S. Department of Education. Washington, DC: National Center for Education Statistics. Retrieved from https://nces.ed.gov/pubsearch/pubsinfo.asp?pubid=2018144.

Mushi, S. 2002. "Acquisition of Multiple Languages among Children of Immigrant Families: Parents' Role in the Home-School Language Pendulum." *Early Child Development and Care* 172: 517–30.

Nagase, Y., and K. Kuramochi. 2011. "Shudanhoiku niokeru asobi to seikatsusyukan no kanren: sansaijikurasu no katazukebamen kara" ["The Relationship between 'Daily Work' and 'Play' in the Kindergarten for Preschoolers: Focus on the Clean-Up Scene"]. *Research on Early Childhood Care and Education in Japan* 49 (2): 73–83.

Rodriguez-Valls, F. 2016. "Pedagogy of the Immigrant: A Journey towards Inclusive Classrooms." *Teachers and Curriculum* 16 (1): 41–48.

Sleeter, C., and C. Grant. 2000. *Making Choices for Multicultural Education: Five Approaches to Race, Class, and Gender*. 3rd edition. Upper Saddle River, NJ: Prentice Hall.

Sohn, S., and X. C. Wang. 2006. "Immigrant Parents' Involvement in American Schools: Perspectives from Korean Mothers." *Early Childhood Education Journal* 34 (2): 125–32.

Suárez-Orozco, C., and A. Carhill. 2008. "Afterword: New Directions in Research with Immigrant Families and Their Children." *New Directions for Child and Adolescent Development* 121: 87–104.

Takanishi, R. 2004. "Leveling the Playing Field: Supporting Immigrant Children from Birth to Eight." *The Future of Children* 14 (2): 61–79.

Villegas, A. M., and T. Lucas. 2002. "Preparing Culturally Responsive Teachers: Rethinking the Curriculum." *Journal of Teacher Education* 53 (20): 20–32.

Winterbottom, C. 2012. "Voices of the Minority: Japanese Immigrant Mothers' Perceptions of Preschools in the United States." *Early Childhood Education Journal* 41 (3): 219–25.

Winterbottom, C., and V. E. Lake. 2013. "Teaching Teachers to Use the Outdoor Environment." In *International Perspectives on Forest School: Natural Places to Play and Learn*, edited by S. Knight, 146–58. London: Sage.

Yaden, D. B., J. Salazar, and D. Brassell. 2003. "The Impact of Spanish/English Language Emergent Literacy Activities during Preschool on First and Second Grade Achievement in English Language and Reading." Paper presented at the American Educational Research Association.

5

CREATING WORLDS FROM WORDLESSNESS IN *THE ARRIVAL*

A Dramatic Dialogic Inquiry Approach to Immigration with Preservice Teachers

Nithya Sivashankar

According to the United Nations High Commissioner for Refugees (UNHCR) report published on June 19, 2018, the world is "now witnessing the highest levels of displacement on record. An unprecedented 68.5 million people around the world have been forced from home. Among them are nearly 25.4 million refugees, over half of whom are under the age of eighteen" (UNHCR 2018). Along with the dramatic rise in the number of forcibly displaced people around the world, the need to inform children and educate teachers about immigrant and refugee experiences in the United States has also increased.

While history textbooks have never sufficiently addressed the complexities of immigrant experiences and have been guilty of misrepresenting and underrepresenting immigrant groups in the United States (Foster 2006), there has been an upward growth in the amount of fictional narratives being published for children and young adults in the past three years (Amos 2018). Picture books and novels about the immigrant experience serve as mirrors to children who have been displaced from home, while also functioning as windows to readers who might not have undergone these trials on a firsthand basis (Bishop 1990).

Lamme, Fu, and Lowery (2004) recommend the use of picture books about immigrant experiences in elementary school classrooms to supplement the social studies curriculum. Apol and Certo (2011) note that verse novels, which are "now part of a wider world of poetry for children" (285), are useful in portraying stories on immigration, a topic that was once considered troublesome. Boatright (2010) proposes the use of graphic novels about immigrant experiences in high school classrooms, and specifically offers *The Arrival* by Shaun Tan (2006) as an example of graphic narratives on immigration that English Language Arts (ELA) teachers can use with their students.

Boatright (2010) puts forth suggestions on how to employ immigration narratives in the graphic novel form in order to engage in critical literacy practices in the high school classroom. While writing about *The Arrival*, a wordless graphic novel, Boatright determines that readers of this "pictorial narrative" (471) come to experience a model tale of the immigrant experience. They get to see the main character overcome major obstacles with determined grit and transform into a "self-made man" (471).

The Arrival offers ELA teachers a great opportunity for questioning the portrayal of immigrant experiences while they argue the merits of good or bad immigrant labels (Boatright 2010). Further, they can grapple with how these labels are determined. This chapter uses *The Arrival* as the focal text to propose a culturally responsive teaching tool for teacher-educators to engender authentic dialogue on issues relating to immigration with preservice teachers who might not be immigrants themselves.

THE PEDAGOGICAL FRAMEWORK: DRAMATIC INQUIRY

Gay and Kirkland (2003) contend that culturally responsive teaching (CRT) practices should be an integral component of teacher preparation and classroom practices. This is of utmost importance for ethnically diverse students. They suggest that it is imperative for teacher educators to provide opportunities in their classrooms for preservice teachers to dialogue with each other about critical racial and cultural issues. Additionally, Gay and Kirkland offer "role-playing and simulation" as a way through which preservice teachers can build their "cultural critical consciousness and self-reflection" (185–86).

Edmiston (2013) proposes the term "Dramatic Inquiry" to describe the active mode of teaching and learning wherein participants engage in dramatic play, dramatic performance, reflection and inquiry in order to experience what it means to take on a fictional character's perspective in the storyworld. This critical literacy practice invites students and teachers to participate in dialogues and inquire, either as "themselves or as if they are other people [in the world of the story being dramatized,] about a topic that is contextualized in a sequence of dramatized narrative events" (180). Dramatic inquiry functions as an effective pedagogical resource for educators to practice culturally responsive teaching in their classrooms.

In the context of immigration, dramatic inquiry allows non-immigrant preservice teachers to occupy the roles of fictional immigrant characters thus providing them the opportunity to assume diverse perspectives on the issue. This, in turn, equips them with the tools required to conduct dramatic inquiry in their own classrooms in the future, wherein they are likely to encounter immigrant students along with citizens. Edmiston (2013) points out that:

> [f]raming young people in dramatic inquiry . . . can provide them with a very different viewpoint from those usually assumed in classrooms where children often have little power to make decisions, influence events, make meaning, or create outcomes that have much value beyond school requirements. (205)

Dramatic inquiry thus serves as a valuable means to encourage dialogue about sensitive issues including immigration, not only with older adults, but also with young children.

By incorporating dramatic inquiry as part of the teaching methods in the classroom, teacher educators can aid preservice teachers in understanding that the imagined storyworld is a level playing field in which students work collaboratively, irrespective of their positionalities in the real world. Edmiston (2013) determines that as young readers participate in dramatic learning, they learn to create and reflect on their shared experiences from their "fictional or factual worlds" (88). This ensures that the classroom functions as a community and meets the learning needs of all students, including their immigrant peers.

THE TEXT: *THE ARRIVAL*

According to Beckett (2013), *The Arrival* is an example of "crossover literature" (1). This subset of literature includes narratives that cross from child to adult or adult to child readers. Beckett (2013) notes that this wordless graphic novel created a new path in the picture book genre, most notably in the crossover picture book category. This graphic narrative by Shaun Tan, which presents the journey of an immigrant in a strange land, positions the reader in the role of a stranger in an unfamiliar place, entirely through the use of surrealistic, monochrome illustrations.

Tan, the Australian author-illustrator, who is a child of immigrants, situates readers—regardless of their age, nationality, language, or cultural knowledge—in a common plane, and provides them the opportunity to embark on the immigrant's journey along with the protagonist. Campano and Ghiso (2011) determine that *The Arrival* is an influential example that presents immigration as an issue for children and adolescents in "ways that make visible its varied characteristics without essentializing the experience into a single narrative or resolving its contradictions" (168).

Several educators and researchers have capitalized on the potential of wordlessness in *The Arrival* and conducted research with K–12 students—both immigrants and non-immigrants—from across the world (for example, Martínez-Roldán and Newcomer 2011). Others have used this wordless graphic novel in the context of teacher education (Graff 2010; Rhoades et al. 2015), and in English and foreign language education, too (Cimermanová 2014; Mathews 2014).

Additionally, there has also been work done on *The Arrival* and drama education (Neelands 2009; Rothwell 2011). Dallacqua, Kersten, and Rhoades (2015) propose arts and drama-based pedagogies as a way to foster "multiliteracies" in K–12 classrooms, using Shaun Tan's novel. As part of the essay, they briefly reflect on the dramatic inquiry work conducted in a third-grade social studies classroom. However, they do not extensively discuss their dramatic inquiry work with the third-graders; neither do they offer pointers to teachers on how to carry out this practice in the classroom.

DRAMATIC INQUIRY AND *THE ARRIVAL*

This chapter provides a detailed lesson plan based on Shaun Tan's graphic novel that could be used to engage preservice teachers in dramatic inquiry in order to bring about authentic dialogue on immigration in the classroom. While it is unclear whether Dallacqua et al. (2015) employ the text-centered or the text-edged approach to drama (Wolf, Edmiston, and Enciso 1997), the latter approach to this pedagogical method is used in order to enhance the dialogic nature of the lesson.

Edmiston and Enciso (2002) state that in the text-edged drama approach, instead of creating a linear dramatization of a story, teachers and their students "*sequence events dialogically* to create dialogue in which discourses come into conflict and meanings can be problematized" (870). In accordance with their framework, and unlike Dallacqua et al.'s (2015) work, this chapter presents a dialogic approach to dramatic inquiry that centers "on the conflict between discourses not merely on the conflicts between people" (Edmiston and Enciso 2002, 871).

As a means of reshaping the text in order to provide the preservice teachers diverse narrative arcs to choose from and build on, the lesson focuses on the endpapers of *The Arrival* (see Figure 5.1) to design the first activity for the classroom. The front and back endpapers feature a grid of life-like illustrations of the faces of people from diverse backgrounds. There are sixty panels in the grid, and each of them, powerful in their own right, tells a story of the immigrant whose headshot is confined to that particular frame.

At the beginning of the lesson, the teacher-educator (for whom a gender-neutral pronoun is used in this chapter) projects the endpapers on to the screen and invites their students to carefully read the images. They subsequently hand out notecards to their students and give them instructions to write a brief story about any one person from the sixty faces depicted on the endpapers. The students can choose to write about somebody who isn't represented in the illustration, too. Once they have completed writing their fictional narratives about the imagined immigrant characters, the educator collects their notecards, shuffles them, and randomly hands out the cards to the students. This ensures that the students do not have the notecards containing the story that they themselves wrote for an imagined character.

Figure 5.1.   Endpapers of *The Arrival* (2006) by Shaun Tan

The second activity in the lesson involves the students embodying the roles of the characters that they have been handed and putting up a dramatic performance under the instruction of the educator. Before proceeding to set up the scene for the performance, the educator invites three or four volunteers from the class and informs them that they will not be playing the characters that they have been assigned. Instead, they will act as immigration officers in the imaginary country, for which the class will come up with a name. The educator then describes the setting for the classroom drama—the airport in the imagined country (henceforth referred to as "Tanland")—and displays to the students the single-panelled page containing the illustration of the crowded immigration queue at the airport in *The Arrival* (24).

The students are then instructed to come up with secondary characters, such as parents, children, spouses, friends, etc., with whom their characters are likely to be traveling. They can choose to travel alone if they want to, as well. The educator then provides a few minutes to the students to think about their roles and the nuances of the same. Some of the questions that the educator might put forth to the students at this point include:

- Are "you" (addressing the students as characters) an immigrant or a refugee?
- Have you been forcibly displaced from your homeland or was it your choice to come to Tanland?
- Where is home? What does home mean to you?
- What is the purpose of your visit to Tanland?
- Who [and what] are you traveling with, and who [and what] have you left behind at home?
- What documents are you carrying with you?
- Do you know where you are likely to be living while in Tanland?
- Are you planning to return to your home country?

While the majority of the students mull over their characters and their stories, the educator has a private conversation with the students who have volunteered to embody the roles of the immigration officers. Here, the educator can make multiple choices. They can: a) provide a handout containing the immigration policy of Tanland to the students-as-officers and instruct them to follow the rules outlined on the document; b) suggest that the students-as-officers come up with an immigration policy for the country themselves and that they produce it in the form of a handout; or c) spend some class time (before the first activity) working with all the students to frame the immigration policy of Tanland.

Once the policy is in place, the students-as-officers are told by the educator that they can only allow a certain number of people into the country, since Tanland has run out of resources to support too many immigrants. It is to be noted that the educator is creating a conflict in this storyworld, as opposed to utilizing an existing tension from *The Arrival*, reifying the text-edged nature of this dramatic approach.

The dramatic performance begins when the students-as-officers take up their respective seats in the classroom and the students-as-immigrants form a queue to get their documents checked and their path to Tanland cleared. Edmiston and Enciso (2002) point out that:

> [a]ll of these inventions of dialogue, interactions, presentations, and plans enable children to participate in the authoring of the text. As they invent and elaborate on the text's potential, they generate multiple

perspectives based on their knowledge of stories and life. . . . These
pathways enable the teacher to actively engage children with the problems of conflicting viewpoints and discourses without taking children
directly to enactment of the moment of conflict [from the textual narra-
tive]. (870)

Through this dramatic performance, the conflicting discourses of the officers and the immigrants come to the fore. The students-as-officers are
faced with making difficult choices, in accordance with the laws of the
land, while the students-as-immigrants turn desperate to become one of
the select few to gain access to life in Tanland. Some of them are allowed
to enter the country while others are rejected and sent to the deportation
cell. The educator can allow the performance to go on until the immi-
grant/refugee quota for the country is met.

The penultimate activity in the dramatic inquiry process is for the
students to participate in reflection as characters in the storyworld. The
educator takes on the role of a journalist who is covering the conflict at
Tanland's borders and questions the officers about the rationale for their
choices. The educator-as-journalist also puts forth questions to the immigrants who made it on the other side of the checkpoint and to those who
were sent back to the deportation cell. The students continue to stay in
character and reflect on their actions, engaging in a dialogue not only
with the educator, but also with their peers. New tensions are likely to
arise during these conversations because as "each context and discourse
is made visible, its meanings reflect and refract the previous presentations" (Edmiston and Enciso 2002, 870).

Once the interview is complete, the educator announces to the class
that they are stepping outside the storyworld into the real world. The class
will finally engage in a collective reflection on the entire process of
dramatic inquiry that they had embarked on, and dialogue around the
topic of immigration at large. A useful way to dialogize the meanings that
arise in these conversations would be to compare the immigration policy
in the storyworld (Tanland) with that in the real world (present-day
USA). The students, having taken on the perspectives of immigration
officers and immigrants/refugees in the storyworld, use their temporary
experiences from the imagined world to dialogue about diverse perspectives on the issues surrounding immigration in the real world.

CONCLUSION

This chapter proffers a pedagogical framework for teacher-educators to help dialogize discourses around immigration in preservice-teacher classrooms. Dramatic inquiry serves as an effective tool for educators to engage in culturally responsive teaching practices. In adopting perspectives that are diverse from their own, educators and students cultivate empathy for people who are different from them. This practice fosters a sense of community in the classroom when students and teachers participate in the dramatic inquiry process together, thus creating a safe and nurturing learning environment.

The issue of immigration is highly topical on a global scale, and it will continue to be so for the foreseeable future. It is imperative that teacher-educators equip preservice teachers with the tools necessary to work with immigrant children in their classrooms. By creating a common ground through the use of fiction and drama, teachers can make their classes more inclusive and engaging for a diverse group of children.

REFLECTIVE QUESTIONS FOR CRITICALLY CARING AND CULTURALLY RESPONSIVE EDUCATORS

1. What roles do you think the educator's positionality and life experience play in this activity?
2. How can this activity be tailored to teach the rhetoric around immigration that prevails in various parts of the world, including the United States?
3. What are the possible means through which the educator can tap into the cultural wealth and experiences of their immigrant students during this activity?
4. Can you think of different ways the educator can involve students who might be reluctant to participate in drama-based activities such as this one?
5. What are the advantages and disadvantages of the educator entering the storyworld along with their students, and enacting the role of a character in it?

REFERENCES

Amos, D. 2018. "New Kids' Books Put a Human Face on the Refugee Crisis." NPR.org, July 10. Retrieved from https://www.npr.org/2018/07/10/626184256/new-kids-books-put-a-human-face-on-the-refugee-crisis.

Apol, L., and J. L. Certo. 2011. "A Burgeoning Field or a Sorry State: US Poetry for Children, 1800–Present." In *Handbook of Research on Children's and Young Adult Literature*, edited by S. Wolf, K. Coats, P. Enciso, and C. A. Jenkins, 275–87. New York: Routledge.

Beckett, S. L. 2013. *Crossover Picturebooks: A Genre for All Ages*. New York: Routledge.

Bishop, R. S. 1990. "Mirrors, Windows, and Sliding Glass Doors." *Perspectives: Choosing and Using Books for the Classroom* 1 (3): ix–xi.

Boatright, M. D. 2010. "Graphic Journeys: Graphic Novels' Representations of Immigrant experiences. *Journal of Adolescent and Adult Literacy* 53 (6): 468–76.

Campano, G., and M. P. Ghiso. 2011. "Immigrant Students as Cosmopolitan Intellectuals." In *Handbook of Research on Children's and Young Adult Literature*, edited by S. Wolf, K. Coats, P. Enciso, and C. Jenkins, 164–76. New York: Routledge.

Cimermanová, I. 2014. "Graphic Novels in Foreign Langage Teaching." *Journal of Language and Cultural Education* 2 (2): 85–94.

Dallacqua, A. K., S. Kersten, and M. Rhoades, M. 2015. "Using Shaun Tan's Work to Foster Multiliteracies in 21st-Century Classrooms." *Reading Teacher* 69 (2): 207–17.

Edmiston, B. 2013. *Transforming Teaching and Learning through Active Dramatic Approaches*. Hoboken, NJ: Taylor and Francis.

Edmiston, B., and P. E. Enciso. 2002. "Reflections and Refractions of Meaning: Dialogic Approaches to Reading with Classroom Drama." Retrieved from https://www.mantleoftheexpert.com/wp-content/uploads/2018/01/edmiston_enciso-dialogic.pdf.

Foster, S. J. 2006. "Portrayal of Immigrant Groups in US History Textbooks, 1800–Present." In *What Shall We Tell the Children?: International Perspectives on School History Textbooks*, edited by S. J. Foster and K. A. Crawford, 155–78. Charlotte, NC: Information Age.

Gay, G., and K. Kirkland. 2003. "Developing Cultural Critical Consciousness and Self-Reflection in Preservice Teacher Education." *Theory Into Practice* 42 (3): 181–87.

Graff, J. M. 2010. "Countering Narratives: Teachers' Discourses about Immigrants and Their Experiences within the Realm of Children's and Young Adult Literature." *English Teaching: Practice and Critique* 9 (3): 106–31.

Lamme, L. L., D. Fu, and R. M. Lowery. 2004. "Immigrants as Portrayed in Children's Picture Books." *The Social Studies* 95 (3): 123–30.

Martínez-Roldán, C. M., and S. Newcomer. 2011. "'Reading Between the Pictures': Immigrant Students' Interpretations of *The Arrival*." *Language Arts* 88 (3): 188–97.

Mathews, S. A. 2014. "Reading without Words: Using *The Arrival* to Teach Visual Literacy with English Language Learners." *The Clearing House: A Journal of Educational Strategies, Issues and Ideas* 87 (2): 64–68.

Neelands, J. 2009. "Acting Together: Ensemble as a Democratic Process in Art and Life." *Research in Drama Education: The Journal of Applied Theatre and Performance* 14 (2): 173–89.

Rhoades, M., A. Dallacqua, S. Kersten, J. Merry, and M. C. Miller. 2015. "The Pen(cil) Is Mightier Than the (S)word? Telling Sophisticated Silent Stories Using Shaun Tan's Wordless Graphic Novel, *The Arrival*." *Studies in Art Education* 56 (4): 307–26.

Rothwell, J. 2011. "Bodies and Language: Process Drama and Intercultural Language Learning in a Beginner Language Classroom. *Research in Drama Education: The Journal of Applied Theatre and Performance* 16 (4): 575–94.

Tan, S. 2006. *The Arrival*. New York: Arthur A. Levine.

United Nations High Commissioner for Refugees (UNHCR). 2018. *Figures at a Glance*. Retrieved from http://www.unhcr.org/figures-at-a-glance.html.

Wolf, S. A., B. Edmiston, and P. E. Enciso. 1997. "Drama Worlds: Places of the Heart, Head, Voice and Hand in Dramatic Interpretation." In *Handbook of Research on Teaching Literacy through the Communicative and Visual Arts*, edited by J. Flood, S. B. Heath, and D. Lapp, 492–505. New York: Simon and Schuster Macmillan.

Section II

Practice and Reflection

6

USHER'S NEW LOOK

Transforming Lives of Immigrant Teens through "Spark" Exploration and Peer-to-Peer Programming

Careshia Moore and Yvette Cook Darby

The status of immigrant youth remains a heavily debated topic in the United States. Many of these youth are among the United States' most socioeconomically disadvantaged youth citizens (Crosnoe and Turley 2011). They are often underserved, do not receive quality education, and are not given the necessary exposure to change their narratives and become thriving adults. Nineteen years ago, Usher Raymond IV realized that he had an opportunity to make a difference with disconnected youth, and so began Usher's New Look, Incorporated (UNL).

Usher's New Look is a 501(c)(3) nonprofit organization that transforms lives of underserved youth through its comprehensive program that develops passion-driven global leaders. Over the past nineteen years, UNL has impacted the lives of over 50,000 youth, ages fourteen to twenty-four, all over the globe. UNL's core programming takes place in Atlanta, Detroit, Milwaukee, and New York City. New York and Georgia are among the two states with the highest population, and the highest increase, of immigrant children living with parents (Migration Policy Institute 2017). This status is reflected in the demographic of teens served in these locations. Approximately 60 percent of UNL's total students served are first- or second-generation immigrants.

Usher's New Look takes on the responsibility to create a flame of hope for all students. This includes students who are first-generation and second-generation immigrants. The students UNL serves are teens who stand at a distinct disadvantage and increased chance of being disconnected from resources outside their academic environment. This results in them being unprepared to navigate the crucial years of middle and high school as a springboard to successful opportunities in college and beyond. UNL starts a spark in the lives of teens—something they didn't know they had—furthering a dream or a talent, making opportunity a reality. UNL makes learning relevant, exposes students to peers that will inspire them, and provides its participants with opportunities to find their future paths.

A Youth Crisis

Usher's New Look operates to alleviate the youth crisis for youth in underserved areas. The youth crisis is primarily centered on education and poverty. In the United States 1.3 million youth drop out of high school annually (Child Trends 2014). Child Trends indicates that low-income students are six times more likely to drop out of high school, while one in five youths lives in poverty. This statistic more than doubles for blacks and Hispanics. Nearly 28 percent of first-generation children and 25 percent of second-generation immigrant youth live in poverty (Child Trends 2014).

The result of these dismal statistics is that students with lower levels of education are more likely to commit crimes and be jailed than their more educated peers. These students seem to have broken lives and limited mindsets regarding success, education, and their futures. These deficiencies and obstacles directly impact students' futures and the outlook of the power they have to operate with a growth mindset.

USHER'S NEW LOOK: THE WORK

Using a peer-to-peer training model, UNL develops students into well-rounded, forward-thinking, and socially conscious leaders. Its comprehensive programming occurs in three phases: Powered by Service; Leadership Academy; and Moguls in Training. The three phases are founded on the organization's four pillars: talent, education, career, and service.

Powered by Service

Young people can often feel powerless and as a result make decisions that derail their success. They may not understand that the skills necessary to become successful adults need to be learned and cultivated at a young age. Interpersonal communication, empathy, critical thinking, and leadership are all skills that may not be emphasized in a traditional classroom, but are necessary for leadership development. During adolescence, the power that peers have over one another becomes strong and can often have a negative impact. Youth need to learn to be confident in who they are and to begin to understand the connection between education, graduation, and becoming a contributing global citizen.

During a six-hour in-school gateway Powered by Service workshop, led by current and former UNL Academy Leaders and Moguls in Training, UNL's college students help students explore their individual "sparks" (i.e., talents, passions); articulate their "personal brand" (i.e., how they wish to be viewed by others); analyze the traits of well-known leaders; explore the root causes of local issues of concern to them (e.g., homelessness, bullying, substance abuse); and make a personal commitment to create and execute Powered by Service projects.

The peer-to-peer workshop spans six hours and provides participants with engaging activities allowing them to discover core tenets of Usher's New Look. Participants experience activities including the following:

- **Networking 101**—participants learn and practice the fundamentals of networking.
- **Personal Assessment**—participants assess their interests, strengths, and passions to explore a variety of "spark" possibilities.
- **Defining Your Brand**—participants assess their current brand and image and understand how they can positively align their lifestyles with their "spark." Participants also explore how personal brands are directly related to social media presence.
- **Leadership 101**—participants identify and discuss the traits of great leaders, consequently discovering which traits they share with the leaders discussed. Participants are also encouraged and empowered to implement the principles that they have learned in their school and the community.
- **Exploring the Issue**—participants are taught how to analyze issues they identify within their communities. They work collaboratively

to analyze an issue, its causes and effects, and to provide potential solutions.

- **Expressions**—participants are provided the opportunity to share their "spark" with peers, support others sharing their "sparks," and demonstrate self-confidence.
- **Financial Literacy**—participants work collaboratively to explore basic principles of financial literacy in a scenario-based format.

These activities are employed with all students and enable them to project their own voices. This format is particularly impactful for immigrant participants who may not reflect confidence in a traditional classroom.

New Look Leadership Academy

One of the primary missions of high school in this modern time is to prepare its students for college and career. Preparing students to compete in a global, information-based economy is the impetus behind the New Look Leadership Academy (NLLA). All students must be equipped with twenty-first-century skills as a prerequisite for success. As academic requirements become even more rigorous for high schools, the focus on skills necessary to succeed such as communication, collaboration, and leadership is diminished. To aid in providing necessary training in these areas, UNL created NLLA.

NLLA is a four-year program experience that exposes high school students to the tools and skill sets necessary to achieve success in their post-secondary education option and career industry that aligns with their passions. Each year, the students are engaged in meaningful experiences through UNL's curriculum, validated by Emory University's Goizueta Business School, and strategic opportunities. The curriculum is designed to provide students with the opportunity to experience each of UNL's four pillars: Talent, Education, Career, and Service. Students prepare for the SAT/ACT, learn how to write successful college applications, navigate the financial aid process, and make plans for college visits and interviews. Corporate sponsors and community volunteers introduce them to a variety of careers through "motivational minute" presentations and job-shadowing opportunities. Through our peer-to-peer training model, youth explore their "spark"/passion, develop leadership skills, mentor younger students, and spearhead service projects in their communities.

NLLA is implemented using two models: the In-school model and the City-wide model. Youth participating in the In-school model participate in the Leadership Academy for high school credits during full-time or part-time participation. A certified UNL Leadership Academy coach facilitates the class. Students also join the City-wide New Look students who meet after school for joint Leadership sessions and extracurricular activities related to the organization's programming.

During each year of the four-year Academy, students participate in activities related to each pillar:

- 9th grade (Talent)—Youth personally assess their "sparks" or talents and engage in activities that allow them to develop, share, and understand how talent can be used in education, career, and to benefit the community.
- 10th grade (Education)—Youth are provided with an in-depth look at the power of education and its use as a vehicle to success. They are equipped with tools that assist in goal setting and navigating the post-secondary education process.
- 11th grade (Career)—Youth participate in a variety of engaging activities that allow them to acquire job-readiness skills. Opportunities are provided to apply the skills obtained in real world experiences including job shadowing, resume preparation, and job interviews.
- 12th grade (Service)—Youth expand their perspective on philanthropy and service through research, interaction with service leaders, and organizing and implementing service projects.

Academy students also attend four "Spark Days" that provide an extended and meaningful experience based upon each of the four pillars: Talent, Education, Career, and Service.

Moguls in Training

Despite widespread access to higher education in the United States, the same level of access is lacking for low-income, minority, and immigrant students. Research has shown that once those students enroll, they experience challenges that result in less success and lower graduation rates than their peers. Lack of relevant experiences, insufficient academic training, and inadequate preparation are identified as factors that inhibit success. Studies have shown that to promote success and graduation students should be: exposed to strategies that ease the transition to college; taught skills that assist with social and academic integration and student engagement; provided feedback on student progress; and be immersed in a culture of success (Tinto 2007).

Using an online curriculum supplemented by interactions with peer- and near-peer role models, New Look's college-aged participants, Moguls in Training (MITs), learn essential skills necessary for them to graduate from college and transition into adulthood successfully. The MITs also lead Powered by Service workshops, travel nationally and internationally, mentor younger students, and gain valuable work experience through summer internships with New Look's corporate and community partners. The program keeps students on track to graduate on time, seek employment, or pursue graduate studies in their chosen fields.

Moguls in Training meet virtually each month to discuss and receive information and resources that lead to college graduation, personal development, productive matriculation on college campus, and successful transition into adulthood. Maintaining the peer-to-peer model, monthly discussions are led by a UNL peer who also employs industry experts where appropriate. Following the monthly session, MITs are provided additional resources to assist with applying the skills gained during the session. The topics explored focus on various areas including: Preparation to Succeed; Tapping into Resources; Developing You; and Getting Ready for the Real World.

IMPACTFUL STRATEGIES: UNL SUCCESS SECRETS

Throughout all the core programs, UNL uses strategies that bring relatability and buy-in to its curriculum. Students begin with "spark" identification through "spark" assessments and exploration. This is important because this is usually the first time that students realize that they should value the gifts and talents they have. This is particularly important in immigrant families where students have been told that they will need to work within familiar industries or family businesses. Essentially, they are forced to ignore the "spark" within them. Exposing youth to their "sparks" opens an entirely new realm of possibilities.

One of the most impactful strategies is the peer-to-peer training model. The entire curriculum is facilitated by peer- or near-peer trainers. These peer trainers are current UNL students or alumni of the program. This model provides for instant relatability between the students and the facilitators. The diverse group of peer trainers is trained to deliver the curriculum and to share their transformation story and "spark" discovery experiences. Students connect organically with peer trainers who relate to them and are inspired by seeing the success of those who look like them, speak the same language, understand their culture, and who are authentic in building trainer-trainee relationships. The peer trainers are trained to be culturally responsive in their delivery.

The curriculum is delivered using innovative and creative strategies combined with experiential and engaging opportunities. It is not uncommon to walk into a session and hear the most current music playing while students are working in cooperative learning groups to complete a project. Trainers solicit students' feedback and input and their peers laud them for their responses. Trainers spend one-on-one time with students to personally connect with the participants. Trainers are taught to build a community to increase student confidence and voice.

Finally, students are engaged in service learning and taught critical thinking skills to creatively solve community issues. UNL is service and community focused. All students are taught to look outside themselves and identify issues within their schools, family, country of origin, and local communities. They are trained to analyze the causes and effects of the issues and determine ways in which the issues may be diminished or eradicated. Many immigrant students have identified government and political forces as an issue. The environment is established in a manner that promotes comfort in sharing ideas and true beliefs. Students acquire a voice to share problems and the courage and power to offer meaningful and tangible solutions that incorporate their "sparks." After every level of the program, participants receive a local certification endorsed by Emory University's Goizueta Business School.

FOCUS AREAS OF TRANSFORMATION

In working to transform the lives of the marginalized youth, UNL has found five focus areas that yield the greatest results in transformation:

1. Growth Mindset—The activities and exposure the students receive lead to a desire for them to achieve higher levels of achievement in their lives. Students are constantly inundated with opportunities, inspiration, and didactic lessons on embracing challenges, persisting despite setbacks, exhibiting work ethic, and embracing feedback. This philosophy, in most cases, is markedly different from the fixed mindset with which these students come into the program.

2. Financial Empowerment—Participants work collaboratively to explore basic principles of financial literacy in a scenario-based format. The success our participants experience through leadership, education, and career will be sustained because they will have gained the necessary tools to live in financial greatness and will become models for others.

3. Education—Participants are provided with resources and guided through creating blueprints for secondary and post-secondary education. Scholarly habits, educational outlook, and the importance of education are relayed to students in a myriad of ways. Students who had not even thought about college often make the choice to go because of their exposure to education opportunities.

4. Self-Efficacy—UNL's program acts as a positive influence on teens' self-efficacy. Bandura proposes that, "Belief of one's self-efficacy is a key personal resource in self-development, successful adaptation and change" (Urdan and Pajares 2006, 4). Self-efficacy is a strong predictor of the life choices that people make. UNL therefore works to help teens understand their potential so that they may succeed in life through increasing their personal agency, providing opportunities to succeed, and emphasizing work ethic in addition to talent.

5. Career Exploration—Through experts, job shadowing, and internship opportunities, students are exposed to various career industries including those that relate to their self-identified "spark." Students are also trained in job readiness skills they may employ as teens and as adults.

CONCLUSION

Usher's New Look has gained concrete results with its culturally responsive programming. The organization has achieved 100 percent high school graduation rate of students who participate in the Leadership Academy. Of the students who graduate high school, 98 percent continue to post-secondary education or career.

The students who have participated in UNL have developed confidence to achieve and a voice to bring about change in their communities. They are armed with knowledge that builds confidence and have gained skills that allow them to network with peers and professionals alike. They articulately express their "sparks" to strangers and advocate for issues they care about. In addition to a change in their speaking, students begin to think differently. A transformation takes place in the way they view themselves and their community.

These students develop a growth mindset that is the catalyst for them taking control of their futures. The unknown becomes possible, and they are no longer victims to other perceptions of them and their race, ethnicity, gender, or socioeconomic status. Throughout the program, students begin to see themselves differently. They see themselves through the eyes of their peers and the stakeholders and mentors they meet. Participation in any phase of the program and its experiences provides a comprehensive infusion of experiences and exposure that changes the participants' mindsets resulting in a different lived experience, thus changing their narrative.

REFERENCES

Child Trends. 2014. *Immigrant Children*. Retrieved from https://www.childtrends.org/?indica tors=immigrant-children.

Crosnoe, R., and R. N. L. Turley. 2011. "K–12 Educational Outcomes of Immigrant Youth." *The Future of Children* 21 (1): 129–52.

Migration Policy Institute. 2017. *Frequently Requested Statistics on Immigrants and Immigration in the United States*. Retrieved from http://www.migrationpolicy.org/article/frequently-requested-statistics-immigrants-and-immigration-united-states#Demographic.

Tinto, V. 2007. *Strategies for Improving Student Retention* [PowerPoint slides]. Washington, DC: The Pell Institute for the Study of Opportunity in Higher Education. Retrieved from http://www.pellinstitute.org/downloads/presentations-Tinto_090607.ppt.

Urdan, T., and F. Pajares, eds. 2006. *Self-Efficacy Beliefs of Adolescents*. Charlotte, NC: Information Age.

7

A NON-IMMIGRANT'S IMMIGRANT EXPERIENCE

Relocating after Hurricane Maria

Carrie Teston Geiger

The student is not technically an immigrant. In fact, he is an American citizen. But, when asked about the word "immigrant" and how it relates to his situation, he uses the word "complicated." He explains that legally, he is not an immigrant but culturally, he is. In his words, his culture is "related to, but separate from, America." Ultimately, in his view they are quite different.

The Storm

Alfredo came to my school after Hurricane Maria. His parents reluctantly left their home in the Puerto Rican countryside so that he and his sister could continue their education. The family returned to Gainesville, Florida, the city in which his father had graduated from law school. Alfredo has vague memories of attending one of the local elementary schools eleven years ago, while his father was attending the University of Florida. After his graduation, they returned to Puerto Rico to be with extended family. This was a choice his father made because of the value and importance of the family unit.

Hurricane Maria descended on Puerto Rico on September 20, 2017, preceded by Hurricane Irma on September 6. While there was significant loss of life on the island, the devastation of the infrastructure was most impactful for Alfredo and his family. The distance they lived from the city meant that they would not be high priority for restoration of electricity, Internet capability, or transportation services.

Alfredo expresses that leaving home is difficult under any circumstances, but it seems especially traumatic in the face of a natural disaster. He says, "Seeing missing houses and cars, as if someone dropped a bomb on everything I had known—that stays with you." He describes his family as being homeless and leaving all of his friends and possessions behind. Additionally, he believes that had he stayed in Puerto Rico, he would never have graduated from high school on time. "If I had stayed, I would have failed, and not from lack of effort," he states.

Because of the damage to roads and other infrastructure, it was extremely difficult for Alfredo to get to school. Rising at 4:00 a.m., he would not arrive at his school until midday or later, depending on traffic. The school day ended at 2:30 p.m., significantly abbreviating his opportunity for study. He would return home, arriving around 10:00 p.m., only to try to complete homework and start all over again on the following day. Being in the countryside meant that he had no electricity; he completed homework by candlelight. He had no access to his online textbooks, anatomy labs, or study guides. He describes walking into quizzes blind, knowing little, if any, of the material. There was no phone reception, so calling a classmate for help was not an option. He feels that he would have been at a big disadvantage had he stayed in his homeland.

Alfredo is a responsible, high-achieving student, so his perceived impending failure caused a great deal of emotional stress in addition to the physiological challenges of limited resources and lack of sleep. He describes the emotional turmoil of other family members as well, especially his father. He divulges, "This was a very traumatic experience in more than one way, and it weighed most heavily on my father, because he sustains the family." In Puerto Rico, Alfredo depended on his parents, but upon arriving in Florida, he realized that "here, they depended on me." While his mother studied business in college in Puerto Rico and his father is a practicing attorney, his parents do not feel confident speaking English. Alfredo became the family translator and spokesperson. This was a "completely different place," both geographically and emotionally, he confesses.

Transition to a "Foreign" School

Alfredo's flight from Puerto Rico provided a learning opportunity—for me as a principal, for our school counselors, faculty, and staff, and for our students. Reflecting on Alfredo's experience, as well as on my own research into immigrant education, elicited a wealth of questions. How do our systems work for immigrant students? Are there things that we did well in this unique situation? What can we do better when confronted with a similar circumstance in the future? I chose to examine Alfredo's experience as a case study in order to analyze our support structures with a view toward continuous improvement.

P. K. Yonge is a Developmental Research School, and as such, its population represents the racial and income demographics of the state; selection of students is conducted through a lottery process, and there are always a number of applicants hoping to matriculate. As one of four Developmental Research Schools in the state of Florida, the school's mission is to design, test, and disseminate promising educational practices while also providing a high-quality educational experience for the 1,155 K–12 students. As a department in the University of Florida's College of Education, P. K. Yonge's seventy-five faculty members are often collaborators with College of Education professors as they conduct classroom research.

We are a single-school school district, meaning that we have no district office and must fulfill state initiatives locally. While this adds a burden to our school-based staff, it also provides some autonomy in how we carry out state mandates. In addition to meeting all the standard requirements of any Florida public school, the state requires that the demographics of our population match Florida's as closely as possible. Therefore, our population of students varies ethnically and socioeconomically to mirror the diversity of our state. Approximately 17 percent of our students identify as Hispanic/Latino. One difference between P. K. Yonge and most other schools in the area is that we do not provide transportation for our students. This guarantees at least a minimal amount of parental engagement, as families are required to transport their children to and from school.

Our school's administrative team is headed by the director, and as the principal, I am assisted by a director of Student and Family Services, a director of program outreach and development, four school counselors, and two behavior support coaches. Our connection with the University of Florida has allowed us to partner with the Department of School Psychology; we have a full-time school psychology doctoral student and a part-time school psychologist on our Student and Family Services team. We meet weekly to discuss systems and evaluate the impact of the work on individual students being served. When our governor announced that enrollment conditions would be relaxed for students relocating from Puerto Rico after the storm, we began to discuss the services that would be needed and how we would accommodate such students if they requested enrollment at P. K. Yonge.

It is under very rare and traumatic circumstances that a student enrolls midway in the semester at our school. Accepting students in a Hurricane Relief effort opened a new territory which had to be figured out as the semester progressed. In conversations with Alfredo I sought to find out what went well for him in the transition and what proved to be most challenging. His story provides insight into areas for celebration as well as foci for improvement in similar future instances.

The curriculum of the school Alfredo attended in Puerto Rico was specially designed to prepare students for college in the United States. This allowed for a smooth transition into P. K. Yonge. His educational record's courses were easily matched with the exception of one course— a Government and Economics class required of all seniors. Like P. K. Yonge, Alfredo's school in Puerto Rico is a K–12 school; however, the school is divided into two separate campuses, with a pre-K through grade six and a seventh- through twelfth-grade site. With only around 200 students, the campus Alfredo attended is much smaller. Architecturally, his school is the combined size of the P. K. Yonge gym and adjacent parking lot.

Attending a sprawling thirty-one-acre campus school with over one thousand students was a big change for him. He recalls, "It was weird seeing people and not getting to know them," and he admits still having difficulty navigating the large school grounds. Seven months after his enrollment at P. K. Yonge, he confesses that he knows how to find his classes and the library, but that is about the extent of his familiarity with the geography of the campus. One challenge for him is that all six portable classrooms look the same.

Leaving a tight-knit community of school friends under difficult circumstances and transitioning into a much larger setting during his senior year proved daunting for Alfredo. Alfredo says that his eighth-grade sister, Andrea, had a much easier time assimilating into the social setting. For one thing, there's more variability in the course selections seniors take; because their post-secondary goals vary, their course progressions are disparate as well. Whereas eighth graders have a more fixed set of classes and therefore more opportunities for peer interaction.

Alfredo explains that there is not as much of a perceived benefit from investing in a new friendship when one is a senior, especially when someone comes mid-year. There will only be a short while to get to know a person before graduation, so the investment of time into a new relationship may not seem as appealing. He expressed that it was much harder to connect with his peers as a senior, because most cliques and peer groups had already been formed by the time he arrived at the school. When asked about his interactions with his sister while at school, Alfredo smiles and says, "We pretend not to know each other."

Because of the relationship I developed with Alfredo over time, I asked if he would be willing to share his transition experiences with me. Thankfully, he agreed to do so, despite the fact that recounting the events was undoubtedly painful. Alfredo points to many things that we, as a school community, did well, including helping him select courses, guiding him through his college application process, the support expressed by his teachers, and the kindness of his peers.

Successes

When asked about the positive ways that P. K. Yonge faculty, staff, and students assisted him in his transition, Alfredo praised the school counselor, who helped him "be at peace with the transition" and who coordinated a schedule that was as much like his previous classes as possible. In his words, "Things that resemble things done in the past helped me retain some sense of normalcy." He also mentions that getting back on a day-to-day schedule kept him from spiraling in the face of his trauma on the island.

Alfredo arrived at P. K. Yonge on Friday, October 27, 2017. It had been decided that he would apply to the University of Florida, to follow in his father's footsteps, but also to keep the family close together after such a tumultuous time in their lives. Applications for the University of Florida were due on November 1. He expresses gratitude for the administrative support which assisted him in timely completion of his application to the university within the limited timeframe. In addition to the support with the application process, our counselor worked with him to establish state residency and thus allowed him to become eligible for reduced tuition. Alfredo had a monthly appointment on the counselor's schedule, but also knew that he could drop by any time he ran into a complication. As a testament to his scholarship, he was accepted to the University of Florida and began classes in the fall of 2018. He plans to pursue dual degrees in Philosophy and Global Studies, with his sights set on attending law school after graduation.

Alfredo mentions that his classmates and teachers treated him very well, that the teachers were understanding of his unique situation and were therefore quite supportive. Interestingly, he credits the positive treatment from his peers to his strong command of the English language. He implies that a student with less English competency may not fare as well. Alfredo describes himself as more of a "literature and language" student as opposed to a "math/science" student, and he indicates that this penchant for language increased his chances for a successful transition into his American school. He also believes that it was helpful that he is outgoing; and, in our conversation, he wondered aloud how an introvert might experience a similar situation.

One of our goals at P. K. Yonge is that every student is involved in some type of extracurricular activity, and Alfredo did not escape this expectation. He was encouraged to seek out activities similar to those he had participated in back home. He selected the Speech and Debate Team, a group he had active participation in at his former school. There was comfort in the familiarity of this activity and he was extremely success-ful, scoring the highest marks at the state level, and representing P. K. Yonge at the national competition in Washington, DC, in June 2018. After the school shooting tragedy in Parkland, Florida, on February 14, 2018, Alfredo sought me out and volunteered to speak at our school safety assembly—evidence of his growing confidence and connectedness to the P. K. Yonge student body.

Spanish class was another safe place for Alfredo. As a native Spanish speaker, he found this class to be especially nurturing and supportive. Sharing a language brings people together, he says, and the P. K. Yonge students who were able to speak Spanish fluently served as a pseudo support system for him. He also became involved in the UNICEF and

Habitat for Humanity clubs, was inducted into the National Hispanic Honors Society, and transferred his membership in the National Honors Society from his former school. Although these activities made his schedule more complex and busy, Alfredo believes that his involvement in the community of his peers kept him from going crazy. In an effort to provide as typical a twelfth-grade experience as possible, the school provided free tickets to Alfredo so that he could attend the Senior Prom. This gesture proved to be quite meaningful for him and let him know how much the PKY family cared about him.

P. K. Yonge seniors are required to complete a capstone project, aptly called the Senior Project. Because of his arrival well into the year, Alfredo was given the option to complete the project or abstain from participating. The project involves research on a self-selected topic, advisement from an expert knowledgeable on the topic, the preparation of a presentation, and the delivery of the presentation before a panel of community-based judges. This is a project that PKY students face with equal amounts of anticipation and dread throughout their high school careers.

Given the choice, Alfredo decided to complete the project. He explains that there was a similar expectation in his former school, and he had already formed the thesis statement for his research in preparation for completing the project there. He verbalizes that this was a tough decision: "I could *not* do it and focus more on other schoolwork. But doing it would give me a greater sense of normalcy and would help me to be the student that I was before the hurricane." He worried that participating in the Senior Project would cause his other courses to suffer, and he was reluctant to be in a situation where he would have to receive help, but in the end, he felt that it was worth it to invest the time in such an important experience, even though he admits that his other grades were, in fact, negatively affected. He explains that, "The Senior Project made me feel a lot more at home than anything else [e.g., the prom], because it restored normalcy that I desperately needed."

Lessons Learned

Much of Alfredo's success as he made the transition into P. K. Yonge is to his own credit as a strong student who was willing to take initiative and be involved in normal senior activities. He was successful despite the challenges associated with assimilation into a class of seniors, many of whom had been in school together since kindergarten. Reflecting on Alfredo's experience and the support we offered, when faced with a similar circumstance, we hope to be more intentional, leaving less to serendipity and the benevolence of our students and teachers, and putting less onus for success on the transfer student himself.

For example, a written plan for involvement in clubs and extracurriculars could be a component of the scheduling conversation. Better labeling of buildings and a clear map should be provided to new students. In addition, a student ambassador who has the same course schedule could guide the student through the first couple of weeks to assist with navigating campus and acclimating to the school culture. While Alfredo easily adapted to the new environment, not all new students would have recovered at the same pace from such a traumatic experience. We have learned that regular counseling sessions should have been extended and provided for him and his sister as a means of helping them process their experience of loss and relocation.

Additional Considerations and Implications

As I reflect on Alfredo's experiences, I wonder if the media exposure to the recent tragedy in Puerto Rico created a deeper sympathy and willingness to help displaced Maria victims. Given the relative invisibility of the children of other immigrant groups, I posit that public sympathy for the relocated Puerto Rican students allowed them a modicum of acceptance that other immigrant students may not receive. In my limited experience with the Hurricane Relief students, I witnessed that our faculty, staff, and student body welcomed them with open arms. This is quite in contrast to the experience of other groups, such as migrant farmworker children. Perhaps the news coverage of the hurricanes that devastated Puerto Rico generated empathy and a sense of altruism among Americans. Perhaps if more were actually known about the experiences of other immigrant groups a greater sense of concern would be fostered for them as well (Vásquez 2010).

As educators in the public school system, it is our responsibility to provide the best possible educational experiences for every child. Awareness that immigrant children encounter a unique set of challenges and experiences is a first step in addressing their needs. Further research and training is needed to ensure that teachers and other school personnel are equipped to fulfill our mission of meeting children where they are and supporting them in their academic and social-emotional development.

Alfredo's experience evokes many considerations for interactions with students in transition from one homeland to another. First, the role of language cannot be undervalued (Olsen 2000). Alfredo is convinced that his command of the English language provided him with a much more successful acclimation into a new school within a different culture. He feels that this made him better able to integrate with his peers and survive academically. Secondly, efforts to provide what Alfredo terms as any possible degree of "normalcy" is critical to reducing anxiety, especially in the wake of trauma. The fact that many of his classes were similar, that he could build his Senior Project off of a comparable project from his former school, and that he could become involved in extracurricular activities somewhat connected to those he had engaged in back home contributed to a sense of familiarity within an atmosphere of strangeness.

Another consideration is the role that sympathy plays in how the receiving country accepts immigrant students. Are there ways to change negative perceptions of the immigrant experience and increase understanding by sharing the stories of individual immigrants? Sharing the personal stories of immigrant children may open a more positive dialogue about the immigrant experience and eventually shift perceptions away from negative stereotypes and discourses of fear. Can we build empathy among faculty and staff through professional learning so that they provide all immigrant students with the same support my colleagues provided to Alfredo?

Finally, it seems crucial that displaced students remain culturally and emotionally connected to their homelands (Waldinger and Duquette-Rury 2016). As Alfredo expresses, "Everything boils down to identity. And while this identity is not only found in extreme circumstances, after Hurricane Maria, I have a lot more pride in my identity. I survived. And that says something about me as a person, from a certain country, city . . . home." Alfredo is proud of his Puerto Rican heritage. He continues to mourn his losses and the separation from his home and friends. It is paramount that receiving schools are intentional about making a time and space for students to celebrate their cultures, and that they offer critical counseling resources so the student can begin to process their grief and trauma.

While Alfredo ended the year successfully and seems to have a bright future ahead, he indicates that he still feels conflicted about being in the United States. He articulates, "While I'm thankful for the opportunity to come to P. K. Yonge and for all the support—they saved me!—at the same time, I feel for my homeland." He explains that this abstract idea of "home" forms a person's identity and creates a patriotism that is integral to a person's being. He says that while Hurricane Maria took a lot away from him—his friends, his home, his belongings—it also gave him insight that he would not otherwise have gained. Hosting a survivor such as Alfredo has accomplished the same for this principal. Alfredo's willingness to share his struggles with me will, I hope, better prepare me for supporting students escaping trauma and other catastrophes. In addition, I will continue to shape the discourse and practices surrounding the student immigrant experiences within my own community of educators. While none of us can be prepared for every storm that arises, as educators, we should at least be equipped to help support students in the period of transition.

Reflective Questions
for Culturally Responsive Teachers Working
with Immigrant Students

1. How might students in my classroom help immigrant students adjust to the changes they are experiencing?
2. What can I do to help the student feel ownership and a sense of efficacy over his/her own learning?
3. What aspects of the student's new setting will be most familiar, and how can these similarities be leveraged to help the student feel more readily acclimated?
4. What aspects of the student's new setting will be least familiar, and what supports can be provided to prevent the student from feeling overwhelmed?
5. What will be the most effective means of communication with the student and his/her family?
6. What types of counseling services does the student need in order to best cope with the social-emotional experiences related to his/her immigration experience, and who will provide these services?

7. What types of career/college readiness counseling does the student need in order to insure the least amount of disruption to his/her matriculation process, and who will provide these services?

REFERENCES

Olsen, L. 2000. "Learning English and Learning America: Immigrants in the Center of a Storm." *Theory Into Practice* 39 (4): 196–202.
Vásquez, M. 2010. "Teaching Students to Consider Immigration with Empathy." *Diversity and Democracy* 13 (1). Retrieved from https://www.aacu.org/publications-research/periodicals/teaching-students-consider-immigration-empathy.
Waldinger, R., and L. Duquette-Rury. 2016. "Emigrant Politics, Immigrant Engagement: Homeland Ties and Immigrant Political Identity in the United States." *The Russell Sage Foundation Journal of the Social Sciences* 2 (3): 42–59.

8

BEING STRATEGIC IN PLANNING

Financial Education for Immigrant Families

Sandra Benain-Reid-McKoy

Immigrants make up a major group of workers in industries in the United States today. Being an immigrant of Jamaican descent and immigrating to the United States of America at eleven years old, I soon learned that a lack of finances would be a hurdle for immigrant children at home, in the classroom, and in society, if they were to be successful. I attended a school where academic achievement was not the focus; rather, the focus was who wore the coolest name brand jeans, name brand shoes, or drove the fanciest cars. Furthermore, your parents' wealth and the zip code you lived in identified your worth.

I was blessed to have parents in Jamaica who cared for me, but I was now living in America. Housing came from my aunt and her family during this time, while financial support came from my parents who lived in a country where withdrawing more than fifty US dollars from one's bank account, at that time, was a criminal offense.

My parents would find any means necessary to get funding to me to help support my living and schooling expenses. They also traveled to the United States to make sure I was cared for and to forego complete dependence on extended family. As a high school student, I worked after school as I adjusted to life in America. Working and earning while in school helped me to realize the importance that money played in the economy and most importantly, in our daily lives.

While attending community college in south Florida, I wrote a paper in my Human Resources Class entitled, "My Goal Is to Become a Financial Advisor." I will never forget the feedback from my professor. Professor Baker (pseudonym) stated, "Financial Advising is a male-dominated industry where neither immigrants nor minorities have much opportunity in this profession." Her feedback was deflating, but also inspiring at that time because I leaned on my faith. I had faith, trusting and knowing God made all things possible. I therefore pursued the career of financial advising, getting the necessary licenses, training, and education to advance my career. I have now been working within the financial industry for thirty-two years and counting.

FINANCIAL EDUCATION AND IMMIGRANT EXPERIENCES

Many immigrant children and their families do not receive financial education in the classroom, financial resources at home, and financial mentorship from the community. Many immigrants struggle when they arrive to this country. They are oftentimes forced to acquire jobs that pay less than or at minimum wage. Many have financial responsibilities back in their homelands where extended family members depend on them for financial support, thus making them a financial contributor to two or more households. As a result, the potential for saving is limited because of the meager wages they initially earn, and expenses often exceed their earning which leads to negative debts.

The lack of available creditworthiness for most immigrant families becomes a major concern. These families take years and sometimes decades to build wealth, as they are unable to secure assets such as purchasing a house, thus disenabling them from building equity early upon their arrival to the United States.

Many immigrant families also suffer from a lack of financial education when they receive their first credit card. Credit cards are often treated as an open checkbook or line of credit, without the realization of the effect of compounding interest that occurs on the balances when consumers take months and sometimes years to pay off the amounts due. When many immigrant families start to build credit, they oftentimes end up in bankruptcy or some type of settlement structure which then ruins their opportunities to receive credit for years to come—due to the lack of education or being fiscally knowledgeable.

FINANCIAL ADVISING FOR IMMIGRANT FAMILIES

In my job as a financial counselor, I have been working with immigrant families for a number of years. It has been rewarding as I have taught clients, including adults and their children, the benefits of not spending all the monies they earn. It is important for families to know what their financial options are, and having solutions to choose from is closely linked to economic prosperity. The success of these families is dependent on the access they have to good quality paying jobs, saving money, purchasing cars, buying homes, access to credit, business building, and the availability of credit. From piggy banks to fixed deposits, saving money is something that most of us try to accomplish throughout our lives. Many families understand the concept of "putting something away for a rainy day" in case of family emergencies.

The envelope philosophy (Ramsey 2012) has been around for decades and is a prime example of the "rainy day" saving. I first learned the envelope philosophy from a Dave Ramsey financial seminar. This system allows you to use cash for different categories of your budget. The cash is kept in labeled envelopes. This allows you to see exactly how much money you have left in a given category by taking a quick peek in your envelope.

I have encouraged clients, families, and friends to use the envelope system for items that tend to eat away at their budget. Some examples of items we can budget for, where the envelope concept can be utilized, include eating out at restaurants, vacation planning and spending, entertainment expenses, gasoline expense, groceries, and clothing expenses. It is important when using the envelope system, to not borrow from other envelopes and shuffle cash from one expense category to fund another (Ramsey 2012). Again, the purpose of the envelope system is to control spending and have a disciplined approach to spending. Moehlenpah (1999), in *Master Your Money or It Will Master You*, also provides practical principles for good money management.

Another trait of saving is giving. If you are able to give, you are able to save. I often ask clients if they are tithers, giving 10 percent of their income to a worthy cause. If they are not a member of a local church, they should practice giving back or contributing to some type of charity. I also encourage families to open a checking and saving accounts. Many immigrant families, or the wage earner, tend to purchase money orders at alternative financial centers to pay their bills, cash checks, or remit monies to their home countries. It is important to build a relationship with a financial institution and seek professional assistance in managing finances.

Immigrant children under the age of eighteen years of age should also establish a minor's savings bank account early and learn the benefits of saving. Many banks and credit unions offer a free account for minors. The minor is able to transition these accounts to their college years and still maintain a fee-free account during this time.

Parents should teach their children checking account skills early in life. Knowing the difference between debit and credit and applying it to balancing one's checkbook or digital reconciling of cash keeps the account holder from overdraft occurrences. Overdraft tends to happen when we are not alert, aware, or active with our financial responsibilities. Parents should also educate their children on the income and expenses of the household so they can be prepared for their future independence.

Many financial institutions will also allow pre-teens to open a checking account with an adult parent/guardian as a joint signor. The continual importance of writing a check or taking advantage of online bill payment is paramount to successful mentorship in the life of an immigrant child and their families. This knowledge should be taught prior to high school or middle school graduations. A checking account is a safer alternative to cash and I advise immigrants that a financial institution is a safe and insured place to put money, write checks, pay bills, and participate in direct deposit.

Many community banks have implemented ways of reaching out to immigrant customers. Banks are marketing remittance products such as money transfer services. They also accept alternative types of identification to make new account opening procedures easier for immigrants. Many banks have also lowered or waived their new account minimum balance requirements to attract depositors.

INVESTING FOR THE FUTURE

A basic education on investments is also vital to growing one's assets as they transition into the American culture. Some basic investment verbiage that immigrants will hear in our media are stocks, mutual funds, trading exchanges, etc.

Stocks

Stocks are shares of companies that are traded on the stock markets. In the United States, the New York Stock Exchange and the Nasdaq are the basic and most popular stock exchanges. Stocks rise and fall on a daily basis, or they fluctuate. These shares represent companies many immigrant families use on a daily basis, for example, many of Walmart's patrons may be immigrants.

Our immigrant children and their families enjoy the products and services of other blue chip companies such as McDonalds, GE, Target, Disney, Nike, Adidas, Apple, Coca-Cola, Wells Fargo, ExxonMobil, General Electric, Samsung, Facebook, Google, Twitter, and the list goes on. Blue chip companies are reliable, and profitable in good times and bad. Stocks have historically produced the highest long-term return although past performance is never indicative of future results. Why don't our immigrant families own a piece of the companies they spend millions of dollars with annually? A lack of financial education is the major cause of this missed opportunity.

Mutual Funds

Mutual Funds are professionally managed pools of money from many investors, used to purchase securities (a tradable financial instrument). They, too, are not federally insured. Mutual funds provide a level of diversification, and liquidity, and professional money managers manage them. Many mutual fund companies offer the convenience of systematically investing with a minimal initial investment of one hundred dollars, monthly. This is a great avenue to secure the lives of our children financially when they get ready for their post-secondary years.

Investing a fixed amount at periodic intervals, regardless of the ups and downs of the market, allows us to maintain a steady course and can be the key to meeting some of our immigrant families' financial goals. Fifty dollars invested at the beginning of every month for twenty years at six percent, would yield the saver/investor $23,217.55. This can be a tremendous investment in the life of an immigrant family's long-term goal.

Bonds

The purchasing of zero-coupon bonds is an alternative investment for parents in saving for their children. These bonds do not pay interest during the life of the bonds. Instead, investors buy zero-coupon bonds at a deep discount from their face value, which is the amount a bond will be worth when it matures or comes due. When a zero-coupon bond matures, the investor will receive one lump sum equal to the initial investment plus the interest. The maturity dates on zero-coupon bonds are usually long-term, and many do not mature for ten, fifteen, or more years.

These long-term maturity dates allow for a long-range goal planning such as paying for a child's college education or affords for a sizable down payment on real property (house). With this deep discount, an investor can put up a small amount of money that can grow over many years. I often advise parents to purchase bonds instead of toys and electronics for birthdays and holiday gifts. Many toys are lying around in garages, discarded by our children. Think of the interest or dividends those funds could be collecting in a financial instrument. It is important for families to evaluate how much they can comfortably put away for the future. Creating a budget is one way to adjust their lifestyles so they can meet the needs of the family.

Education

I have helped immigrant parents to be active advocates in the school life of their children. We live in an era where time is of the essence, hence we have to create time and prioritize our goals whether they be short-term or long-term goals. Showing up at school functions, staying in constant communication with our child's teacher are important steps in this regard.

Educators are an integral part of an immigrant child's educational development. I encourage parents to seek feedback and/or guidance, and most importantly to employ good listening skills for the benefit of our children. Further, immigrant parents can help to make the educator's experience with our child a positive one. The educator can see that the immigrant parent has stake in the well-being of their child's school plans, and is encouraged to engage with the parent for the benefit of the child.

In sharing the importance of education, I encourage families to start a college funding plan. The child may choose not to attend college; however, this asset that can be transferred to another sibling or the parent can also use this account if they decide to pursue their higher education. A 529-college plan provides future tax-free benefits for your child.

Credit

I am a strong advocate in teaching children about the system of obtaining and managing credit. Having and maintaining a credit card is an important step in building their credit history. Using this credit card strategically and paying their bill in a timely manner prevents excess spending and unnecessary debt. Teaching children the importance of working hard and saving for the future will help them to be more fiscally responsible adults.

Summer is a time when many of our immigrant children are bored and feel disassociated. This is a good time to encourage them to get a part-time job or volunteering experience. These experiences will build life skills, and keep them busy, as they develop a greater appreciation for work and helping others. Many civic organizations have numerous volunteering opportunities that students are able to secure for experience and knowledge.

CONCLUSION

It is important that those who are firmly established in the lives of immigrant families and their children (for example, educators, pastors, and community advocates/leaders) learn about their cultures. Understanding the reasons families immigrate can be a start to helping them acculturate to the new cultures. A familiarity with the cultures can also ensure that families receive help before they are overwhelmed by stressful situations and experiences.

Educators and community advocates can have a positive voice in the lives of immigrant children and their families. Communicating with the parents of immigrant children and giving positive accolades about a student can go toward establishing a good relationship with the student and their family. If language is a barrier, educators can solicit the help of the student, or other available resources, in translating an email or a note home into the native language.

Immigrant children should be given the opportunity to speak about their immigration experiences in the classroom. It would be admirable if educators could lend additional help outside of the classroom or solicit local religious communities to do the same. Educators can teach immigrant families the power of social media, helping them to network with others. Advice or legal seminars about their rights living in America, basic health care, and housing are also beneficial for the families.

A well-known truism states: "People truly don't care how much you know until they know how much you care." Many immigrants come to America wanting the same things as immigrants across history. They seek a stable income, an opportunity to succeed, and a better life for their children and their families. Immigrant children bring diversity to our classrooms, our communities, and our country at large. School and community leaders are well positioned to assist the families as they learn to maneuver their way in their new home.

EDUCATION AND COMMUNITY RESOURCES TO HELP IMMIGRANT FAMILIES

The school is a beacon in any community. Immigrant parents send their children off to school because they know they will receive the education they need to succeed in the future. Schools, local churches, and community resource buildings can also provide resources for parents in myriad ways:

1. Provide workshops where parents can learn about acquiring vocational skills, for example plumbing, carpentry, and cosmetology.
2. Invite local business owners to share about resources immigrant parents would otherwise not gain access to (for example, the Boys and Girls Club, local housing authority, or libraries).

3. Conduct regular financial seminars where parents can learn about budgeting for household expenses, short-term goals, and long-term goals. Specific sessions with a bank/financial advisor can provide details on saving and investing, smart borrowing, understanding interest rates and terms prior to signing contracts for car purchases, credit cards, or any type of loan.

4. Highlight schools' curriculums and help parents understand how they can contribute to their children's educations in this new environment.

REFERENCES

Moehlenpah, A. 1999. *Master Your Money or It Will Master You*. Doing Good Ministries.
Ramsey, D. 2012. *Dave Ramsey's Complete Guide to Money: The Handbook of Financial Peace University*. Brentwood, TN: Ramsey Press.

REFERENCES

9

BRIDGING THE GAP

Using Emphatic Intentions to Connect
with the Displaced Immigrant

Angie McDonald

Hardships often prepare ordinary people for an extraordinary destiny.
—C. S. Lewis

In my line of work and exposure to working with and advocating for various at-risk and displaced individuals, I've encountered those who have been resistant or incomprehensive to the level of intention and care that can be provided to them. There are many speculations that can be derived from this type of response or reaction. As a daughter, sibling, and family member of many immigrants, I've had firsthand experience of not being able to freely express any other emotion other than strength and/or resilience in the face of all adversity or oppression.

Call it pride, if you will, or lack of emotion; I've always been puzzled why there was this stigma against seeking out any help or assistance from someone other than our own family member or fellow countryman. As I matured and evolved into my career and line of work, I've taken a serious look at my own reactions to help, empathy, or pure intentions that were directed toward me and/or my children. To better shape this outlook, I'll provide a general overview of my own experience that sheds light on this revelation of what I do as a Transitional and Empowerment Professional, and the methodology behind it.

EXPERIENCE TAUGHT WISDOM

My life experiences granted the knowledge, skills, and abilities to effectively provide the services I currently do. I was widowed at age twenty-eight, in November 2009, with two young children (an infant of three months and a two-year-old toddler). This kind of sudden trauma was not heard of nor experienced in my close-knit cultural community. It took everyone around me by surprise, and left them to constantly feel for words, expressions, and ways to effectively support me in my time of unbearable grief. Having to deal with both post-traumatic stress disorder (PTSD) and postpartum depression, I spiraled into bouts of over-compensating my indescribable grief with "acts of strength," resistance to the process, and irrational decisions.

The flow of events that surrounded my late husband's illness and eventual passing, hardwired me even further to mask my own emotions, and to take on roles and demeanors that gave no room to the necessity of having to process the grief and loss of my beloved life partner and father of my children. It also segued into me not readily being able to grasp the overwhelming levels of support and genuine concern displayed by family, friends, and strangers, alike. I respectfully acknowledged each gesture, but I emotionally and mentally responded in ways that would preserve my stance in maintaining the strength and poise of a woman who can smile in the face of loss and adversity.

In retrospect, I realized that it was not easy for me to handle such kindnesses. I would either take offense, or be upset with myself for getting to this "state of neediness" and disadvantage. It was with my own struggle of pride, willingness to prove my strength and resilience, not to mention internalizing the never-ending rhetoric from my community to "be strong," that sent me into an unhealthy stance of an ineffective and stagnant frame of mind that stunted my recovery, growth, and healing.

This written work will emphasize the unusual stigma attached to helping those from Afro-Caribbean or West Indian countries who are victims of circumstances surrounding grief and loss, imprisonment and reentry, and progressing outside of their "norm." You will find the firsthand culturally responsive pedagogical framework methodologies I had to customize and implement in order to effectively provide ideal services of care, coaching, support, and restoration.

A LOOK BACK—PERSONAL AND HISTORICAL CONTEXT

In order to understand why this kind of approach needs to exist, one must begin to understand the background of the culture of Afro-Caribbean immigrants. Laced with trials and triumph, the Afro-Caribbean experience aligns in many ways with the African American experience, but it also differs in distinctive ways. In exploring my own genealogy and traditions in Jamaica, I've come to understand that there is an ingrained and heightened sense of cultural identity and pride amongst its people, regardless of region, parish, or township.

Jamaicans, especially those with close African roots (respectfully referred to as the Maroons), celebrated themselves as being the ones who confronted European slavery and colonialism, and fought strategically for their independence. Their history began with an attempt to completely enslave them by their British captors once the island was taken from Spanish settlers in 1655. These Maroons or "Cimarrones" were mountaineers who navigated the mountainous Jamaican terrain with ease, which made it very difficult for their European captors to catch up with, much less enslave them. This prowess, coupled with a heavy resistance to slavery, lead to a series of retreats and treaties that ensured the Maroons' freedom and independence to live the lives for which they earnestly fought. This resilience is a major part of the cultured characteristics that makes up the Caribbean immigrant, pretty much regardless of their island of origin (Benitez 2000).

My maternal bloodline directly stems from the Maroons, which opened my eyes to many of our family's traditions, mannerisms, and handling of different struggles. I've observed from adolescence to adulthood the pride and strength that my family (immediate and distant) has portrayed. The unwavering posture of self-control, calm reactions, and even a "hushed" style of talking during a family crisis, death, major loss, or dispute has always intrigued me. I never knew if something was awry after disheartening news was shared, since it rarely outwardly affected the adults in my family. However, as stated before, this strength and resilience, along with pride, has been the staple characteristic of many Caribbean nationals who have encapsulated the role of self-reliance and independence, even in the face of adversity or the help needed to overcome it. I learned to identify with my culture, and made it my own when life's experiences played their usual assertive and disruptive roles in my life.

CULTURALLY RESPONSIVE COACHING
AND IMPLEMENTATION

In my experience working with at-risk, disadvantaged, or emotionally distressed immigrant families and individuals, I've had to incorporate not only personal emphatic approaches to break through to a realm of trust and understanding, but it also required that I be consistently intentional with the methods used. My practices varied depending on the type of service or help needed. Whether it was specific group coaching, intense accountability sessions, or one-on-one discovery sessions, an intentional and personal method to "reach" clients had to be established prior to engaging. If this isn't established and met, the chances of connecting and really making a positive impact with clients will be very slim.

The following personalized responses to real-life interactions I've had with individuals, families, and groups will outline the organic types of services, approaches, and the culturally responsive pedagogy (CRP) that I found to be ideally effective. I've been met with various responses ranging from general initial interest, to deep emotional and personal breakthroughs resulting in progressive movements that eventually inspired others to powerfully embrace the new changes and transitions with anticipation of impactful growth.

Observe and Learn

As a life, grief support, and transitional life coach, I find it essential to be intuitive to the circumstances surrounding individuals who find themselves in difficult times. After all, that is the basis of our training. However, this applies to anyone in a position of assistance, outreach, or with resources to be of support to immigrants and their families. Be mindful that these individuals have to learn to absorb and adapt to the new environments that will undoubtedly come as a cultural shock to their usual way of life.

In addition to having to absorb the norms of a new location, in times of hardship, tragedy, or assimilation, they have to eventually submit to the outside services available to them, which will most likely feel very uncomfortable and uncertain. These uncertainties will bring them to the usual "knee-jerk" response: to instinctively depend upon one another, especially if they have migrated to a community with fellow countrymen or a similar cultural structure. If located within one of these communities, I encourage all those willing to be of support, encouragement, education, or servitude to intentionally observe and learn the ways and cultures that are prominent around them.

Acknowledge and Respond

Acknowledge the pride students or clients may exude, which will most times resemble resistance or apprehension. With keen observation, try to respond with empathy and understanding associated with their fears, and assert yourself as intentional, pure, and willing to assist. My positive interactions have always involved my experiences that afforded me the ability to tune into the emotions leading to an open and ultimately effective response to the needs.

Acknowledging with an emphasis in the *knowledge* of who you are availing yourself to help is an integral part of opening the portal to creating productive and rich dialogue. In this medium, the opportunity to connect, engage, and inspire will be the beginning of a healing journey toward growth, accountability, and promise.

Tell Your Story

It is with an assured level of assumption that those utilizing and engaging in culturally responsive pedagogy and its similarities are doing so with some level of compassion and purpose to educate and inspire. This expression of compassion should also be assured with a personal history that accompanies the intention of bringing a sense of focus and hope. Sharing the lows, highs, and everything in between creates a conduit of genuineness and humanity that will universally connect the displaced or discouraged immigrant(s). It also ascertains that someone with the intent to make a difference, has had some experience with overcoming hardships, grief and loss, or diverse challenges, and is now using the lessons to be of help and/or guidance.

I have personally had to infuse some parts of my story into every session or conversation. I am cognizant of which parts to include and what to leave out (based on my audience), but this is what being a sensitive coach or an effective listener generally entails. It does require tapping into who you are serving and getting a clear preliminary sense of the needs at hand or risks involved. With each encounter, I have ensured to hold myself accountable to the task of sharing my own trials, debacles, and triumphs in humility, coupled with a surety that qualifies me to share in the extent I have been trusted to share. Creativity seals the methodology in which all educators or community advocates will successfully inspire their clientele and/or community.

In day-to-day observation, one can ascertain that the rhythm of immigrant communities communicates a story of uprising, strength, and persistence. Even in the hardships they may face, the willingness to obtain the "dream" of overcoming any obstacle faced has to be acknowledged and respected. Even in their need to seek help, those offering the help must be sure to learn, observe, and respectfully acknowledge their story and the mannerisms involved. This uniqueness is what builds strong communities. Providing intentional and responsive methods of support and transitional care will create the portal to making even stronger communities.

> I had to learn this [repeatedly] until it stuck. I could not have come to the point of sharing, being open and transparent to share my gifts, talents and ideas with people unless I had the experience to prove it. Outside of certifications, affiliations and degrees, I pay homage to the difficult and challenging life circumstances that allowed me to intrinsically understand and embrace the culture of the same individuals I now serve (the widows/widowers, at-risk, underserved immigrant, etc.). I could not passionately relay my intentions to serve, be an advocate voice or point of reference for these individuals, unless I was in fact one myself. I knew firsthand what measures had to be taken or consistently followed up on. [Growing up in a Caribbean culture] I knew what mindsets and attitudes that either had to be taken on or dismissed in order to successfully master the circumstance at hand. Patience indeed was and is virtue. It, coupled with gratitude, were my two most trusted confidants of sanity and productivity. I learned over time to be truly grateful for what I did have, as opposed to what I did not. (A. McDonald, LinkedIn 2016)

REFERENCES

Benitez, S. 2000. "Maroons in Jamaica: Their Origins and Development." Retrieved July 31, 2017, from http://scholar.library.miami.edu/slaves/Maroons/individual_essays/suzette1

.html.

McDonald, A. 2016. "The 'IT' Factor: Be the IT in Invest." [LinkedIn Article, January 1]. Empowerment, training and facilitation guide to providing intentional and effective coaching practices. https://www.linkedin.com/pulse/factor-invest-angerette-angie-mcdonald.

Section III

Resources

10

RESOURCES ON IMMIGRANTS AND REFUGEES

Mary Ellen Oslick, Marla Goins, and Shawn Anderson Brown

According to the US Department of Education, over 4.7 million foreign-born individuals are currently enrolled in pre-K to post-secondary education, which is about 6 percent of the total student population. Another 20 million students are the children of foreign-born parents. As the immigrant population steadily increases, so does the need for schools and communities to support their immigrant students and families (Lowenhaupt and Montgomery 2018). Providing support serves the dual purpose of assisting the families and fostering a cooperative home-school relationship. The following digital resources have been compiled and briefly summarized as supports for immigrant and refugee students and their families.

WEBSITES

Ethiopian Tewahedo Social Services (ETSS): http://www.ethiotss.org/.

ETSS is a nonprofit organization that serves US immigrants and refugee, based in central Ohio. ETSS responds to the cultural assets and needs by providing services in multiple languages, and by promoting public awareness of the diverse, rich cultures ETSS comprises. ETSS hosts services for youth, adults, family care, and mental health, as well as new American integration. Its youth programs include a multi-site after-school program, cultural enrichment classes, summer enrichment camp, and summer employment program. Adults may participate in ETSS English for speakers of other languages courses, job skills training, and citizenship classes. Adults may also benefit from ETSS housing, health care, legal, and translation and interpretation services. Through the Family Care Program, families may learn about domestic violence, sexual assault, and human trafficking, and ways to advocate against, prevent, and get help in response to those crimes. The New American Community Collaborative organizes legal efforts against cyber and verbal harassment, and interfaith dialogue among immigrant, non-immigrant, and long-time resident groups.

The Florida Immigrant Coalition (FLIC): https://floridaimmigrant .org/resources/.

FLIC is an alliance among over sixty legal, farmworker, student, grassroots, and service organizations in the state of Florida. FLIC leads campaigns for immigrant rights and provides online toolkits for beginning new chapters of those campaigns. "Say Yes!" aims to propel an innovative Congress immigration policy, which would facilitate the citizenship of 11 million noncitizen immigrants. "CCA (Corrections Corporation of America) Go Away" challenges for-profit detention of immigrants and non-immigrants. "Drive Safe Sunshine State" advocates for all Floridian drivers to be eligible for a driver's license, regardless of immigration status. FLIC posts regular "Citizenship Drive" events, where immigrants can obtain free assistance with applying for citizenship. The website also displays educational resources, including a list of immigrant-eligible scholarships.

Immigrant Legal Resource Center (ILRC): https://www.ilrc.org/civic-participation.

ILRC collaborates with immigrants, grassroots organizations, and the legal sector to provide legal assistance to immigrants and to impact immigration law. ILRC was initially founded as the Golden Gate Immigration Clinic in 1979 in response to US immigrants' need of organized legal support. ILRC trains attorneys, paralegals, and community activists to provide that support. ILRC areas of expertise include: asylum; citizenship and naturalization; crimes; DACA/DAPA (Deferred Action for Childhood Arrivals/Deferred Action for Parents of Americans and Lawful Permanent Residents); enforcement; immigrant families; immigrant youth; LGBT; removal defense; post-conviction relief; obtaining U Visa; VAWA (Violence Against Women Act); and T-Visa. This website includes a list of ILRC partnerships; books and trainings; podcasts on current events in immigration; manuals for obtaining visas and citizenship; access to ILRC social media outlets; and the biannual newsletter, "The Immigrant Advocate."

Children's Defense Fund (CDF): http://www.childrensdefense.org/.

Children's Defense Fund (CDF) is a private, nonprofit organization that advocates children's access to education and health care. It was founded in 1973 following the Civil Rights Movement, and has since aided in passing over thirty federal Acts for child rights programs, including those for legal protection, vaccines, food and health services, and immigration rights. CDF provides culturally responsive education and training programs for youth and young adults. The following programs are for children: Beat the Odds, for high school students of underserved communities who display exemplary academic success; and CDF Freedom Schools, a summer literacy program. CDF leads campaigns centered on child rights: Road to Freedom; Protect Children Not Guns; Cradle to Prison Pipeline; Be Careful What You Cut; and Black Community Crusade for Children (BCCC). CDF provides an online toolkit for each of these campaigns, for individuals or groups to create their own chapter of a campaign.

CASA of Maryland: http://wearecasa.org/.

CASA of Maryland, Inc., is a nonprofit Latino and immigrant advocacy organization based in Maryland. CASA campaigns for immigrant rights; sanctuary cities; the Affordable Care Act; police accountability; raising minimum wage; undocumented immigrant driver's license eligibility in Virginia; and the Trust Act in Maryland.

CASA provides child and adult education programs including English for Speakers of Other Languages. It also provides work training and employment placement. It houses a Department of Health and Human Services, which consists of legal services, citizenship assistance consultations, health and social services, and financial literacy courses. Its other departments include the Department of Politics; Communications; and

Community Development Initiatives; Schools and Community Engagement; and Community Organizing.

CASA conducts research projects to learn about the communities it serves and how it may best respond to their assets and needs. CASA employs a research-to-action method, in which it brings its research findings to practical use. From a research study on the Langley Park Promise Neighborhood (SOMOS Langley Park) funded by the US Department of Education, CASA developed guidelines for improving immigrant children's readiness for and retention in schooling institutions.

Through the project Learning Together, funded by the US Department of Education, CASA collaborates with public schools and the University of Maryland to research how immigrant parents may successfully navigate the US education system, despite language and education barriers. While parents learn to navigate the US education system through the Learning Together project, they ultimately become active engagers in their children's education, leading their own projects, such as Parent Teacher Organizations (PTOs).

US Department of Education: "Educational Resources for Immigrants, Refugees, Asylees and other New Americans," https://www2.ed.gov/about/overview/focus/immigration-resources.html.

This web page, sponsored by the Department of Education, is dedicated to providing information and resources for immigrant, refugee, asylee students and families. Included among the resources listed are language assistance services; Deferred Action for Childhood Arrivals (DACA) educational resources; guides for parents and teachers of early learners; migrant student education resources; and materials for Hispanic and Asian American and Pacific Islander (AAPI) students. It should be noted that this web page is dated—the welcome message is from former Secretary of Education, Arne Duncan, and refers to former President Obama's immigration policies.

Esperanza Immigrant Rights Project: https://www.esperanza-la.org/.

Esperanza Immigrant Rights Project is a public interest legal organization serving immigrants in the Los Angeles area. According to their website, they teach, defend, and empower children and adults by giving them the tools they need to navigate the complex immigration system. Their Community Education Program is designed to inform immigrants about their rights and possible forms of relief; they also provide assistance to released youth (and their custodians) and detained adults. Additionally, they list attorneys that represent youth in immigration removal proceedings free of charge.

Vera Institute of Justice (ICH): https://www.vera.org/projects/immigration-court-helpdesk.

The Immigration Court Helpdesk (ICH) program educates non-detained immigrants in removal (deportation) proceedings about the court process. The goal of ICH is to help individuals in immigration court proceedings make informed decisions about their legal cases. Vera works with five nonprofit legal service providers, who offer sessions about the immigration court process generally and potential defenses from removal. The program, funded by the Executive Office for Immigration Review (EOIR) and administered by Vera, operates at five immigration courts in California, Texas, Illinois, New York, and Florida.

Stanford Libraries: "Immigrants and Refugees in Books for Children and Young Adults," http://library.stanford.edu/guides/immigrants-and-refugees-books-children-and-young-adults.

This website is an extensive collection of children's books and young adult literature about the experience of immigrants and refugees. It has a link for books recently received that have been published within the last two years. There are also elementary, middle school, and young adult literature sections. Unique to this resource is the inclusion of the Lexile measure. It also features a service (e.g., WorldCat) to locate books at a local library.

BLOG

Pragmatic Mom: "Undocumented Immigrants in Children's Books" and "Modern Immigration and Refugee Experience," http://www.pragmaticmom.com/2013/07/undocumented-immigrants-in-childrens-books/ and http://www.pragmaticmom.com/2017/05/immigration-books-kids/.

This blog, co-written by a librarian, offers extensive lists of multicultural books. Two of the lists may be of significance for those working with immigrants and refugees: "Undocumented Immigrants in Children's Books" and "Modern Immigration and the Refugee Experience." The lists include brief summaries of each book from the publishers or Amazon. These books can be used to teach empathy and compassion.

PDFS

NYU: Steinhardt: "Resources for Immigrant Students and Post-Secondary Access," http://steinhardt.nyu.edu/scmsAdmin/uploads/004/488/resources_immigrant_students.pdf.

This three-page PDF from NYU: Steinhardt gives a list of resources for teachers on how to help students maneuver the complex maze of post-secondary education. It shares information to help students identify financial aid resources, general information, and array of organizations that can help students pursue higher educational dreams.

Health in Schools: "Partnering with Parents and Families to Support Immigrant and Refugee Children at School," http://www.lacgc.org/pdf/PartneringSupportImmigrantChildren.pdf.

This fifteen-page PDF supported by the Robert Wood Johnson Foundation, documents the fifteen sites across the United States that are developing model mental health programs to engage schools, families, students, mental health agencies, and other community organizations to build effective, easily accessible services for children and youth. Centers are located in cities such as New York, Chicago, Los Angeles, Boston, and Raleigh, North Carolina.

CONCLUSION

While this list is by no means comprehensive, we hope that it can provide some supportive resources for immigrant and refugee families, as well as those who are working with them.

REFERENCE

Lowenhaupt, R. and M. Nicholl. 2018. "Family Engagement Practices as Sites of Possibility: Supporting Immigrant Families through a District-University Partnership." *Theory Into Practice* 57 (2): 99–108.

ABOUT THE EDITORS
AND CONTRIBUTORS

ABOUT THE EDITORS

Ruth McKoy Lowery, PhD, is professor of children's literature and literacy, and associate chair of the Department of Teaching and Learning at The Ohio State University. Her current research focuses on immigrant and multicultural literature, the adaptation of immigrant and at-risk students in schools, and preparing teachers to teach a diverse student population. She has published numerous articles and book chapters, and authored/co-edited several books including *Immigrants in Children's Literature* (2000). She is active in the National Council of Teachers of English (NCTE), Children's Literature Assembly (CLA), and the United States Board on Books for Young People (USBBY). Her motto *"Just Read"* encapsulates her love of books and belief in sharing great books with readers of all ages.

Mary Ellen Oslick, PhD, is assistant professor of literacy and reading at Stetson University in DeLand, Florida. She teaches undergraduate and graduate courses in reading methods, children's literature, and critical literacy practices throughout the content areas. Her research areas of interest include social justice and critical literacy applications, multicultural children's literature, and reading and writing instruction with diverse learners. She is an active member of the International Literacy Association (ILA) and currently serves on the award selection committee for the Notable Books for a Global Society (NBGS).

Rose M. Pringle, PhD, is associate professor in science education in the School of Teaching and Learning at the University of Florida. Her research agenda extends into two parallel, yet related research areas in science teacher education. In one line, she focuses on the development of science teachers' disciplinary content knowledge and the impact of professional development on their learning. In her other line of research, she investigates pedagogical content knowledge as a framework for shifting practices to heighten teachers' stances toward issues of social justice and their roles in positioning learners who are traditionally underrepresented in science—of special concern, the participation of girls of African descent in science and science-related careers. She therefore operates at the nexus between what knowledge teachers need and how it becomes translated into effective and culturally relevant practices that challenge assumptions and the status quo and lead to increased participation of all groups of learners in science.

ABOUT THE CONTRIBUTORS

Sandra Benain-Reid-McKoy is a financial advisor specializing in retirement planning with Citi Personal Wealth Management. She earned the professional designations of Certified Retirement Counselor. She has more than thirty years of financial management experience and advises on the development and implementation of investment strategies to help clients meet their immediate and future goals. She consults on risk management, retirement planning, estate strategies, and other critical financial strategies. Sandra is a native of Jamaica and currently resides in South Florida. She earned a BS degree in business management at Florida Atlantic University. Sandra enjoys reading, spending time with family, and being involved in her church community.

Shawn Anderson Brown, PhD, is currently professor of education at Reinhardt University in the Price School of Education, where she has been a faculty member since 2003. Shawn completed her PhD at Florida

State University and undergraduate degree studies at Florida A&M. Her research specialization is in English Language Learners, science, human development, and differentiation. She enjoys working with preservice and in-service teachers.

Yvette Cook Darby is an executive coach, consultant, and philanthropist who has dedicated much of her life to helping people reach their dreams. She has spent over twenty years working with various nonprofits including Usher's New Look and The United Way of Greater Atlanta, to improve the quality of life for those most in need. Yvette is passionate about eradicating poverty, ensuring social justice, equal access to quality education, equal rights, and equal pay. She has a master's degree in communications from the University of Denver, and serves on several community volunteer boards.

Carrie Teston Geiger, EdD, is the principal of P. K. Yonge Developmental Research School at the University of Florida, a lab school with the mission to design, test, and disseminate promising educational practices. After teaching elementary school for twenty years, she joined the administration of P. K. Yonge, first serving as an assistant principal of Instructional Practice. Carrie has worked extensively with preservice, beginning, and in-service teachers to develop and implement best practices focused on increasing student engagement and achievement. She has served as an adjunct professor for the University of Florida College of Education for over ten years.

Marla Goins is a PhD candidate in the Department of Teaching and Learning at The Ohio State University. She is currently doing her dissertation in Brazil as an exchange student at the University of São Paulo. Her research explores the impact of the contemporary activism of afro-Brazilian women on the identities and sociopolitical orientations of afro-Brazilian women preservice teachers. She teaches courses in Linguistic Diversity in Education and Equity and Diversity in Education in traditional and online settings. She has served the activism-based literacy program Freedom School as an intern, site coordinator, and project director.

Christina Levy. As an agent of inspiration and faith, Christina Levy's work emphasizes the importance of owning one's identity and living on purpose. Born in Mandeville, Jamaica West Indies, and immigrating to the United States at age seven left young Christina doubting the power of her voice. She took to writing to combat years of self and cultural silencing which led her to eventually speak out about racially infused violence, education, and her faith. She has performed throughout Northern New Jersey, at Yale University, and Seton Hall University, where she graduated with a bachelor of arts degree in creative writing and psychology.

Arati Maleku, PhD, is currently an assistant professor in the College of Social Work at The Ohio State University. Her research focuses on (a) understanding social determinants of health inequities at the intersection of gender, race/ethnicity, and class in the migration context and (b) exploring pathways to build community resilience and improve well-being among vulnerable communities in transition. Her professional background encompasses over ten years of social work practice, experience both nationally and internationally. Dr. Maleku engages in community-based research projects using mixed method research approaches. She is interested in culturally grounded research and development of culturally grounded measures and culturally responsive interventions.

Angie McDonald, a board-certified grief support and transitional life coach, is CEO of iAM Consulting, LLC and Wounded2Wonderful Coaching. She provides collaborative expertise in assisting, training, optimizing, and preparing our underserved, at-risk, and immigrant communities through various motivational and professional efforts. Her professional expertise, spanning twenty years, and real-life experiences allow her to have an affinity with those who are aware of their calling, profession, and purpose, but are thwarted by circumstances, lack of resources, and information. Her motivational stance provides all whom she engages with the resources and tools to pursue their goals. Her transitional coaching provides supportive and insightful strategies to make the next level most rewarding. Her coaching motto is "Let us grow from Wounded2Wonderful."
Website: www.iamconsultingllc.com.

Careshia Moore, Esq., is the interim president and CEO of Usher's New Look. In her current role, she provides strategic leadership to the organization that develops underserved youth into passion-driven leaders. A lifelong educator, her observation of the disparities among underserved youth was the catalyst for the work in which she is currently engaged, and propels her to continue to seek out innovative strategies to equip youth to compete to succeed. Careshia earned a master's of education and juris doctor from the University of Florida. She is also the author of a children's book.

Justina Ogodo, PhD, is a postdoctoral researcher in STEM education in the Department of Teaching and Learning at The Ohio State University. Her research focuses on science curriculum and instruction, STEM teacher pedagogical content knowledge, and urban education/culturally responsive teaching. She uses her experience to provide preservice teachers with effective tools to prepare them for the profession. She mentors early career teachers through induction programs and provides targeted professional development to enhance in-service teachers' content knowledge and pedagogical skills. In addition to presenting peer-reviewed papers at annual meetings of several professional associations, she has authored two book chapters and some articles.

Sudarshan Pyakurel is a member of the Bhutanese Community in Columbus, Ohio, and is a former refugee from Bhutan. He is the current executive director of Bhutanese Community of Central Ohio (BCCO) and community leader and advocate for social justice. He is also on the board with the Asha Ray of Hope and the founder of the Bhutanese American Students Organization (BASO), founder and managing director of *Jagaran*, a Nepali newspaper published through Columbus, OH. He has a master's degree in English literature and bachelor's degree in economics from India; bachelor's degree in cultural anthropology from The Ohio State University; and associate degree in philosophy from Cuyahoga Community College.

Nithya Sivashankar is a PhD candidate in the Literature for Children and Young Adults program at The Ohio State University. She has an MA in writing for children from University of Central Lancashire, UK, and has worked as an editor at a children's publishing house in India. Her research interests include South Asian and Middle Eastern children's literature, refugee narratives, picture books, and transformative pedagogy. She was awarded the 2017–2018 Rudine Sims Bishop Scholarship for Research in Children's Literature. She has published in *English Teaching: Practice and Critique* (2016), and her essay on the Sami people has appeared in the nonfiction anthology *Life Beneath the Northern Lights* (2014).

Binaya Subedi, PhD, is associate professor in education and human ecology at The Ohio State University. His research examines broader issues of migration and citizenship. The research addresses the challenges and possibilities that immigrant and refugee families create when they collectively migrate across national and international borders. He has published numerous journal articles on topics such as global representations, visual culture, and immigrant youth identities. He is co-editor of the *Educational Studies* journal. His current work includes developing community-based leadership programs within marginalized communities that have faced trauma and violence.

Christian Winterbottom. Originally from Manchester, England, Christian is assistant professor at the University of North Florida. He earned his BA degree in English at the University of Bedfordshire in England, and his master's and PhD degrees in early childhood education at Florida State University. For four years, he taught preschool in Japan. He worked with preschools and Head Start programs and was director of Child Care Training and Accreditation in Florida, where he ran a contract for the Department of Children and Families. He teaches undergraduate and graduate courses in early childhood education. His research focuses on working with marginalized populations, and on reconceptualizing early childhood pedagogy through praxeological learning methodologies.

www.ingramcontent.com/pod-product-compliance
Lightning Source LLC
Chambersburg PA
CBHW020356270326
41926CB00007B/452